Bristol
in old picture postcards

by Andrew Palmer

European Library ZALTBOMMEL / THE NETHERLANDS

Acknowledgements:

The illustrations in this book have been reproduced from originals in the author's private collection. I should like to thank Michael Williams and Lionel Reeves for allowing me the use of their library of local history and for their help and encouragement during the preparation of the text.

About the Author:

Andrew Palmer was born in Bristol and educated at St. George Grammar School. He subsequently attended the University of Hull, and obtained an Honours Degree in Law. Since 1968 he has worked for the Bristol City Council and is presently employed in the Housing Department as a Principal Officer.

GB ISBN 90 288 2491 x

© 1983 European Library – Zaltbommel/The Netherlands

Second edition, 1997: reprint of the original edition of 1983.

INTRODUCTION

Anyone who wished to form a collection of picture postcards which illustrated Bristol as it is to-day would soon realise that although views of the City Centre and the major landmarks such as the Cathedral and the Cabot Tower are readily obtainable, there is precious little additional material available to them at present. This was not always so, because at the turn of the nineteenth century from the approximate period 1900-1918 there evolved what is often termed 'The Golden Age' of the picture postcard, when in addition to the beautifully produced general subject cards, literally thousands of different local view cards were on sale in post offices and newsagents, illustrating every aspect of life as it was at that time.

The craze for sending and collecting postcards was already well established on the Continent. In Great Britain the abandonment by the General Post Office of its monopoly, brought about by a change in the regulations which permitted the use of adhesive stamps on postcards, and the introduction of the divided back which enabled the picture to cover the whole of the other side, provided the stimuli for a number of firms to commence postcard production. Nevertheless many cards were still printed abroad in view of the superior quality of the foreign, especially the German, production methods then in use. From their inception in 1869, postcards had always been sent at the lowest postal rate, in Great Britain a halfpenny, and as the photographic card found greater favour in this country than on the Continent, the local photographers found a ready market for their products.

Great social changes were also taking place at this time. The advent of the electric tram, Bristol being the first city in the country to electrify its hitherto horsedrawn system, enabled a large number of people who had previously been confined to the inner city areas, to travel further afield and to live in the suburbs which were developing rapidly. It was no longer necessary to live so close to ones place of work, and the new housing areas which were in the main of superior quality and design with improved amenities, began to replace the poor quality workmens dwellings built around the factories and other places of work.

The City of Bristol, historically second only to London in commercial importance, expanded greatly during the last quarter of the Victorian era, and the population almost doubled between 1871 and 1905. A series of boundary changes, commencing in 1835, brought a number of parishes and villages within the revised city limits. There was large scale private housing development in areas such as Brislington, Horfield and Knowle, which lost their rural appearance as more open land was built upon.

After the First World War, obligations placed upon local authorities by a succession of Housing Acts led to the creation of large council housing estates in Fishponds, Sea Mills, and the remainder of Horfield and Knowle, at locations set in a broad band some three to four miles from the centre of the City.

The developments referred to, the personalities and events of the time, were all recorded on contemporary picture postcards. Fred Little was busy producing a whole series of cards from Victorian photographs illustrating streets and buildings in the old City which were disappearing even in his lifetime, and which most people now living may never have seen. He also produced a fine series of contemporary views illustrating Edwardian Bristol. Other local photographers such as John William Garratt and Edward C. Stevens were selling postcards of street scenes and events, which were of far superior quality to the majority of cards available from the large commercial suppliers.

It may seem strange to us, that for example, a view of an otherwise empty side street should have been a viable product for a local photographer to have sold. However, apart from the actual collecting of postcards which entailed sending cards showing 'our house' or 'our street' to friends and relations and receiving a similar type of card in return, it should be remembered that prior to the use of the telephone and the private car becoming so widespread, the picture post-card provided a cheap, efficient and speedy method of communication (once it was accepted that the postman and the servants might not after all have either the time or the inclination to read the message first), so why not use what was an attractive, personalised piece of postal stationary.

It is quite common to find a message on a postcard which has been delivered locally, to the effect that the sender will or will not be able to come to tea that afternoon; a tribute to the postal delivery service which in the Bristol District coped with 72,400,000 items of mail in 1905 compared with 30,000,000 items just over a decade earlier.

However, in 1918 the postal rate for sending a postcard was doubled to one penny. The number of cards sent declined rapidly and as a consequence the number and quality of the cards produced also declined. The collecting boom was over. Nevertheless some fine examples of topographical Bristol postcards were issued in the 1920's and the 1930's by Garratt and Hepworth.

Following the outbreak of the Second World War and the consequent effect of air raids upon the city, in particular six major attacks which destroyed much of the central area and parts of the suburbs, the picture postcards which still survive are an even more important visual record of streets and buildings which might otherwise have remained very much the same today.

As interest in the collecting of picture postcards has revived, so the topographical card has once again come into its own, without as yet any general improvement in the quality or variety of the contemporary material which is available. Research into the background of particular local photo-graphers and the series of cards they produced is still in its infancy in most cases. At least it is now appreciated that the many finely detailed items that they issued for sale provide the present collector or local historian with an invaluable and often unique pictorial record of the City of Bristol's con-tinuous development, of its citizens who have long since passed on, and of a City which has in many places changed out of all recognition.

BIBLIOGRAPHY

Christopher Robinson, *A History of the Bristol Hippodrome (1912-1982)*
John Latimer, *Annals of Bristol*
J.O. Symes M.D., *A short history of the Bristol General Hospital*
T.H.B. Burrough, *Bristol*
Reece Winstone, *Bristol as it was (series)*
G.F. Stone, *Bristol as it was and as it is*
Kathleen Barker, *Bristol at Play*
Robert Wall, *Bristol Channel Pleasure Steamers*
edited by Reece Winstone, *Bristol's History*
John B. Appleby, *Bristol's trams remembered*
R.A. Buchanan & M. Williams, *Brunel's Bristol*
Arrowsmith, *Dictionary of Bristol*
F.C. Jones & W.G. Chown, *History of Bristol's Suburbs*
H.E. Meller, *Leisure and the changing city 1870-1914*
Avon County Planning Department, *Railways in Avon*
W. Ison, *The Georgian Buildings of Bristol*
A.H.N. Green-Armytage, *The Story of Bristol Zoo*
Clare Crick, *Victorian buildings in Bristol*

1. The Clifton Suspension Bridge is Bristol's most famous landmark. The concept of a bridge across the Avon Gorge became more realistic when it was feasible to build a suspended form of structure rather than use masonry arches. In 1753 a Bristol merchant, William Vick, left the sum of £1,000 as the nucleus of a fund to build a bridge across the Avon from Clifton Down. By 1830 the estate had accumulated to £8,000, and a proposal for a suspension bridge designed by the engineer I.K. Brunel was accepted at an estimated cost of £57,000. In 1831 Lady Elton turned the first sod, but work subsequently stopped when the Bristol Riots broke out. Five years later on 27th August 1836 the Marquess of Northampton laid the foundation stone of the buttress on the Somerset side but work was abandoned in 1843 when £40,000 had been spent. Brunel did not live to see the bridge completed as he died on 15th September 1859, four years before work to link the towers commenced.

Clifton
Suspension Bridge
nearing Completion

2. When the task of building the Suspension Bridge was halted in 1843, the iron work, including the suspension chains, was sold off to recoup some of the expenditure incurred by the Bridge Trustees. In 1861 a new company was formed which acquired the towers and approaches for £2,000. The sum of £35,000 was raised and work restarted in November 1862. Chains had been purchased from the Hungerford Bridge, London, which Brunel had completed in 1843. A third chain was added to each side of the bridge, the chains being embedded 70 feet into solid rock. Work was completed in 1864 and the bridge was opened on 8th December of that year by the Lords Lieutenant of Gloucestershire and Somerset. From first to last the construction work cost nearly £100,000.

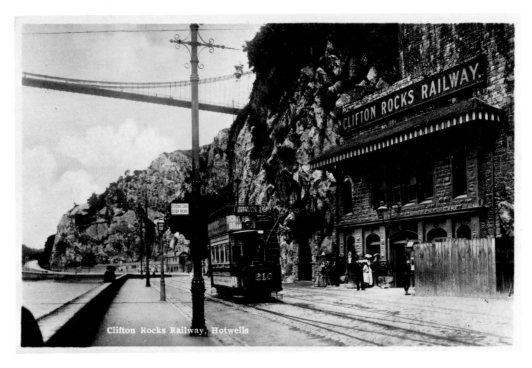

Clifton Rocks Railway, Hotwells

3. The Clifton Rocks Railway was opened on 11th March 1893 linking Hotwells to Clifton and carried about 100,000 passengers during the first six weeks of operation. It was acquired by the Bristol Tramways and Carriage Company on 29th November 1912 for £1,500 and closed in 1934 following continued deficits. A horse tram service ran from the City Centre to Dowry Square, Hotwells commencing on 24th June 1880 and was shortly afterwards extended to the Suspension Bridge; the journey lasted sixteen minutes. By 1898 the tram lines ran from Arnos Vale to Hotwells, and the route was electrified in its entirety by the end of December 1900. Tram No. 210 was one of a batch which came into service in 1900/1901. In the distance can be seen the Bristol Port Railway and Pier Company Station which was in use from 6th March 1865 to 19th September 1921. The buildings were demolished 18th March 1926. The trams also provided a link to the nearby landing stage for the Campbells Steamers which began in 1887.

The Clifton Rocks Railway. ICS&CO 291.

4. It was in 1890 that the Merchant Venturers gave Sir George Newnes permission to excavate the tunnel through which the Clifton Rocks Railway was constructed. The work took two years and cost over £30,000 compared with the original estimate of £10,000. The tunnel is 500 feet long at a gradient of over 1 in 2 and was fitted with four pairs of rails. An 18 seat tram type saloon body was attached to a base which incorporated a water tank. Each pair of cars was connected by steel cables, the weight of the descending car pulling up the other car to which it was attached. If both cars were equally loaded or if there were more passengers in the bottom car, the ballast tank was filled with sufficient water to counterbalance it and set both cars in motion. The 500 feet journey took 40 seconds, the interior of the tunnel being lit by gas lamps. In 1905 it cost 2d. to ascend, but if a ticket was bought from the conductor on Hotwells tramway the cost was 1d.

ROWNHAM FERRY.
BRISTOL. 79.

5. A ferry is known to have existed at Rownham since Norman times and as the Avon could at one time be forded by horsemen, some form of crossing would have been in use prior to that. Before 1870 the ferry was further down river, and at low tide it was possible to cross on a bridge of boats. In 1148 the ferry became the property of the Abbot of St. Augustine's Monastery and subsequently ownership passed into the hands of the Dean and Chapter of Bristol Cathedral. The latter, in 1866, sold their interest to the Bristol Corporation for £10,000. When the Ashton swing bridge was opened on 4th October 1906 it was thought that the Rownham ferry might close. However, despite a fall in passengers it remained popular as a convenient crossing point until its use discontinued on 31st December 1932.

Old Drawbridge

6. The Centre of Bristol as it appeared about 1885 when the Floating Harbour continued towards the Stone Bridge. The Drawbridge was erected in 1868, and was one of a number of different bridges built in succession on the same site. 'Q' shed, the large stone building to the right of the drawbridge, was built in 1879 and demolished in 1892. The tramway system was extended to the Centre on 4th December 1875 following an extension of the track from the Colston Street/Perry Road corner to the Drawbridge. A horse tram service from the Drawbridge to Hotwells (Dowry Square) opened on 24th June 1880. The two horses waiting by the waterside would have been used to assist the pair drawing the tram to pull it up the slope to College Green.

7. The Drawbridge on the City Centre in 1890. Even with horse transport the bridge is a bottleneck as a small cart passes a horse-drawn tram. Controversy over the question whether or not to have a fixed bridge on this spot resulted in at least one change of mind by the City Council before the Drawbridge was closed on 17th May 1892 and the river permanently covered over. Looking up Clare Street, Thornleys hat shop is on the left-hand corner. It was demolished in 1902. In front of the entrance to 'Q' Shed to the left of the nearest tram is a watchman's box which was removed prior to February 1892 when a temporary structure was built to replace the Drawbridge. The old system of The Watch was brought to an end in 1836 and a new police force created, partly because some of the watchmen were 'worn out servants of Members of the Corporation' and others were actually suspected of carrying out the crimes they were supposed to prevent.

DRAWBRIDGE BRISTOL IN 1890   68
BRISTOL   THE DRAWBRIDGE. 203.

8. Following the City Council's decision to replace the Drawbridge with a fixed bridge, the harbour was culverted from the Stone Bridge (Rupert Street) to the junction of Clare Street/Baldwin Street. The work started on 11th May 1892, the last brick being laid by the son of the contractor on 6th May 1893. A former Mayor, Sir Charles Wathen, and others decided to organise an Industrial Exhibition to be built on the space created by the culverting. A wooden building 520 feet long and 110 feet wide was erected at a cost of £11,000. In the southern part were mechanical and industrial exhibits, and in the northern part pictures, sculpture, china and other works of art. The Exhibition was opened on 28th August 1893 by the Mayor, Mr. R.H. Symes. It closed on 31st January 1894 having made a profit of £2,271 which was divided amongst the principal medical charities. The clock on the front of the building was the first in Bristol to be operated by electricity.

9. About 1908. St. Michael's Hill looking down at the junction with Perry Road and the upper floors of the shops at the top of Colston Street. In the distance the spires of Christ Church (City), and St. Nicholas stand on either side of the towers of Temple Church and All Saints (City), with the dome of the Robinson Building (destroyed in the Blitz) visible to the right of the latter. Colston's Almshouses, seen on the left going down the hill, were founded in 1691 for the benefit of pensioners who must have lived in the City for twenty years and be of the Church of England. The wide raised pavement and the street furniture make this one of the most attractive thoroughfares in the City even though the view over the latter has since changed considerably.

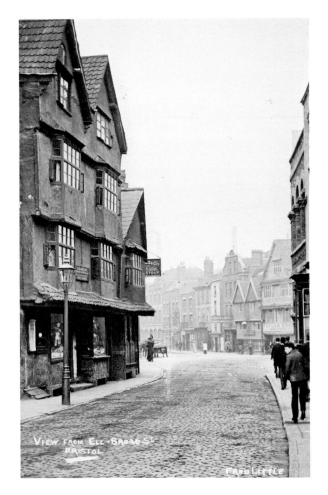

VIEW FROM ELL·BROAD S^T
BRISTOL

FRED LITTLE

10. About 1906. Ellbroad Street connected Broad Weir and Careys Lane, joining with Redross Street and Haberfield Street. This view is taken looking towards Broad Weir, with Lower Castle Street joining where the cart is standing on the left hand side. The half-timbered house seen in Broad Weir on the extreme right was destroyed in 1942. By 1905 the cost of lighting the streets with gas lamps, such as that seen outside the building on the left, was £15,000 per annum. Bristol's principal streets were lit by gas as early as 1817, and the Bristol Coal Gas Company which was incorporated in 1819 was the second such company formed in England. Ellbroad Street disappeared when the Broadmead shopping area was developed.

11. The corner of Old King Street and Milk Street about 1912. The building at the rear is Ridley's Almshouses founded by Miss Ridley in 1739 to provide for five males and five females who had to be either bachelors or spinsters. The almshouses were blitzed in 1940 and demolished in 1954. The old street pattern has disappeared in the redevelopment of the Broadmead shopping area. The watchman's box was built in 1820. Each of the wards in the City had a night constable with a number of watchmen under him. However, large areas were without a single lamp or watchman, resulting in the formation of vigilante groups and the eventual reform of the system of law and order. This particular watchbox was subsequently used as a tobacconist's shop. It was demolished in 1913.

Mary-le-port St

Horton Bristol

12. St. Mary-Le-Port Street was an extremely narrow thoroughfare which connected the central part of High Street with the centre of Dolphin Street, the latter being situated at the top of Union Street. In old deeds the street is called St. Mary de Foro or St. Mary of the Market. Barnard and Company, tobacco, snuff, and cigar warehouse, is seen from Cheese Market, a lane which ran through to Wine Street. The premises were demolished on 9th February 1904. At the time the photograph was taken, about 1900, tobacco was 2d. per ounce and Wills' Gold Flake were 2d. per packet of twenty. Before the earlier demolition of some of the houses in the 1860's it was almost possible for persons leaning from the upper stories to touch each other across the street. Following the air-raids of 1940 St. Mary-Le-Port Street was destroyed, and was not rebuilt.

13. No. 9 Wine Street, birthplace of the poet Robert Southey. His father and uncle had a drapers business on the premises where he was born on 12th August 1774. He married Edith Fricker whose sister married Samuel Taylor Coleridge. Southey became Poet Laureate in 1813; his poetry is little read today. He also edited the works of Bristol's boy poet Chatterton. To the left of Southey's house is Grand Hotel passage, and above it the offices of the Bristol and District Beer, Spirit and Wine Trade Protection and Benevolent Association. Numbers 9 and 10 Wine Street were demolished in 1915 and replaced by Boots the Chemist in premises called Southey House. The latter was blitzed and the road has since been set back. The modern block of shops and offices called Southey House is not on the site of No. 9. Southey had a patron, Joseph Cottle, who not only published his works but even paid for his wedding ring and marriage fees. His shop still stands on the corner of High Street and Corn Street. The fireplace from Southey's house is now in the vestry of Christ Church (City).

14. The Pithay, seen here in 1880, ran from Wine Street along a route very similar to the present, except that it crossed over Fairfax Street and emerged in Broadmead at a point where the rear of the Odeon Cinema now stands. Looking up the hill, the road bends to the left before emerging into Wine Street. The roadway was once called Aylward Street after an important local family. The word Pithay is derived from *puit,* a well, and *hai,* an enclosure of stone. At one time the locality was fashionable but decayed into a rundown area with a reputation for crime. In March 1897 work began on the demolition of the houses, the site being used for an extension to Fry's Cocoa Factory. The latter having moved to Keynsham, the factory premises were demolished and office blocks were built on either side of the road.

15. Prince Street dates from about 1700 and was named after Queen Anne's husband, Prince George of Denmark. The Old Assembly Rooms, which were situated on the corner of Assembly Room Lane, were completed in 1755. Numerous concerts were held there and the buildings were the focus of Bristol Society until the Clifton Rooms opened in 1811. Following internal alterations they became the Regency Theatre, but closed after a period of two years having faced strong opposition from the nearby Theatre Royal. For many years it was used as a warehouse before being acquired in 1909 by the Great Western Railway. It was demolished to ground floor level by 1916. The lane at the side led to Dean's ferry which operated between Narrow Quay and Canon's Marsh. A modern office block has been built on the site, including the sites of the buildings seen on the right of the picture.

OLD ASSEMBLY ROOMS,
PRINCE ST BRISTOL.

FRED LITTLE
COPYRIGHT
488

Tram Centre, Bristol

16. The Tramway Centre in 1899. The triangular area in the centre of the picture, close to the camera, was known as 'Skivvy's Island' in view of the large number of cleaning ladies that used to gather there to catch the trams back from their place of work. The tramway system was not fully electrified until the end of 1900 so there is still a majority of horse-drawn trams in view. There is also evidence of the activities of the street water carts which were required to help keep the main thoroughfares clear of the effects of horse-drawn transport. A ship is drawn up alongside Dublin shed, behind which stand the properties shortly to be demolished for the construction of the C.W.S. building. On the right of the picture the Hippodrome has yet to be built where Smith and Company's premises can be seen, behind the clock on the offices of the Tramways and Carriage Company.

The Tram Terminus, Bristol.

17. The Tramway Centre in 1902 looking from 'Skivvy's Island' to the Clare Street/Baldwin Street junction. Clare Street, begun in 1770 and named after one of the then Members of Parliament for the City, Lord Clare, was the main thoroughfare to the City Centre via Bristol Bridge before Baldwin Street was opened in 1881. The trams are now completely electrified, those on the left going to Hanham and Horfield, that on the right to Brislington. Thornley's hat shop has been demolished and the new Sun Fire and Life Insurance offices (architect, Sir George Oatley) are under construction. These were in turn demolished in 1971 and replaced by a modern office block. The road pattern around 'Skivvy's Island' has now been altered, the areas where the trams are standing having been paved over.

Tramways Centre, Bristol
No. 291

18. About 1908 looking across the Tramway Centre to Colston Street. Farrows Bank, 'The People's Bank', was offering facilities for savings bank deposits from 1/- upwards at 5% interest. All current accounts in credit were kept up to date on a daily basis. The bank building was replaced by a modern tower block in the 1970's. To the left of Farrows is the Bristol Gas Company Building, erected in 1906, demolished and replaced in the mid-1930's. The clock on the Bristol Tramways and Carriage Company's offices was one of several which were controlled to Greenwich mean time by an electric current via the Bristol Goldsmiths Alliance Clock on College Green, the latter being one of two Bristol clocks having a direct connection via the telegraph with Greenwich Observatory. The horse taxis were replaced by motor cars in 1908, the fare being 8d. per mile (first mile one shilling). The Bristol Tramways Company Ltd. had taken over the Bristol Cab Company Ltd. on 1st October 1887.

19. About 1913, St. Augustine's Parade and the Hippodrome. The latter was built on the site of Smith and Company home furnishers whose premises were at No. 13, St. Augustine's Parade; the development of the theatre buildings at the rear removed an area of poor quality residential property in Hanover Street. The architect was Frank Matcham who had undertaken improvements to the Prince's Theatre in Park Row. The Hippodrome opened on 16th December 1912 with a variety programme headed by Eugene Stratton. Also included was a spectacle called Sands O'Dee which made use of the 100,000 gallon water tank revealed when the back section of the stage lifted to allow the front portion to slide back. The first full length talkie to be seen in Bristol was shown here in September 1929. A fire destroyed the rear portion of the building on 18th February 1948; following renovations it was reopened on 24th December 1948. The tower above the facade was removed in 1964.

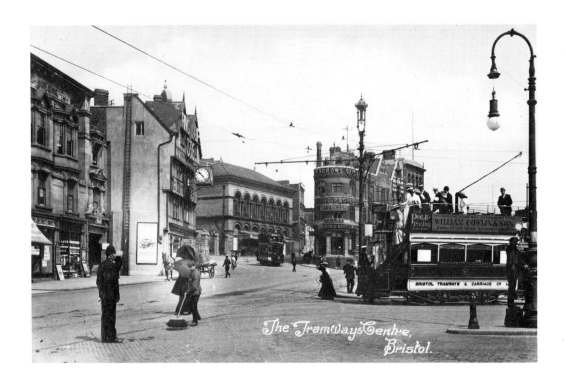

The Tramways Centre, Bristol.

20. Looking towards the Colston Hall about 1911. The buildings immediately behind the tram were demolished in 1970. The YMCA is not yet built in Colston Street. The workman on the right is attending to the electric street lamp. The supply of electricity to private consumers started in Bristol in August 1893, in addition to which 96 public street lamps were connected. The latter had increased almost ten-fold by 1905. During the era of horse transport, the cleaning of the City's streets was a major undertaking. What was then referred to as 'scavenging, ashing, and street watering' had been undertaken by the Corporation since 1892. There were some 331 miles of highway to keep clean and the workman to the right of the policeman was one of some 540 on average directly employed on the various cleaning tasks. Principal thoroughfares like the City Centre were swept daily and throughout the day; other roads were swept two or three times a week or as the weather required.

Colston Hall, Bristol.

21. The Colston Hall 1912. On the extreme left the end of the Gas Company offices, since replaced by a later building. To the right hoardings mask the area subsequently occupied by the YMCA building. The first Colston Hall was built in 1867 at a cost of £40,000. On 1st September 1898 fire from an adjoining clothes factory spread and burnt the main hall. A new hall designed by Hall-Jones and Cummings opened on 27th November 1900; Sir William Henry Wills Bart. gave £5,000 for a new organ. The advertisement at the entrance is for the thirteenth Bristol Musical Festival, a triennial event which started in 1873. The festival should have been held in 1911, but was postponed so as not to clash with the Coronation of King George V. Clara Butt took part in the programme, and although there were notices everywhere about no encores, it was clear when she sang her first song that the orchestra stands had accompaniments for her series of encore pieces. The windows on the upper floor have been filled in and form one side of the Little Theatre which opened on 17th December 1923.

Clare St, Bristol. 112

22. Clare Street, looking from the Tramway Centre towards Corn Street, with All Saints Church opposite the Old Council House. On the right, the premises of D. Glass and Company, tobacconists, stand on the corner of Clare Street and Baldwin Street. The Sun Life Assurance offices on the left were built on the site of Thornleys hat shop and lasted from 1902 to 1971 when a more modern building replaced the one illustrated. In March 1928 the corner was adapted to form a shop, first let to Rothmans the tobacconists. Behind the sign for 'Parsleys' is the main entrance to the Clare Street Picture House, built in 1912 and demolished in 1927. Although once a main thoroughfare to the Tramway Centre and a part of the processional route on great occasions, Clare Street is now a quiet cul-de-sac with no vehicular entry onto Broad Quay.

ANCIENT MONEY TABLES, OR NAILS
CORN ST. BRISTOL. FRED LITTLE

23. About 1904. Looking along Corn Street towards Wine Street in the far distance. The foundation of the Exchange building on the right was laid on 1st March 1740 by the Mayor Henry Combe, the opening being on 27th September 1743. Starting in October 1813 a corn market was held there every Tuesday and Thursday. It was also the appointed place until 1870 for the nomination of Parliamentary candidates and for the declaration of the polls. The four Brass Pillars or Nails were used by merchants in lieu of tables for making payments or writing letters. One came from the Tolzey in front of the old Council House and three from the Tolzey alongside All Saints Church. Two of the nails date from the sixteenth and two from the seventeenth century. At least three were private gifts to the City. Corn Street has now been pedestrianised, the statue in the niche has disappeared and Wine Street was blitzed in the Second World War.

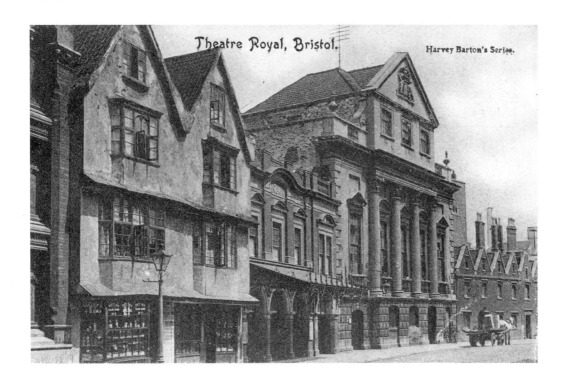

Theatre Royal, Bristol.

Harvey Barton's Series.

24. The foundation stone of the Theatre Royal was laid on 30th November 1764 and the building opened on 30th May 1766. There was great opposition to it especially from Quakers who threatened criminal prosecution against anyone acting in an unlicensed theatre. The building was influenced by the design of Wren's Theatre in Drury Lane, London, except that the auditorium is in the shape of a horseshoe. The interior was altered in 1800 when the ceiling was raised to form a gallery. The entrance shown is by Pope and Skinner and was built during 1902. The houses on the left were demolished in 1903. To the right of the theatre is the Coopers' Hall, built in 1743 and used for many years as a fruit warehouse and auction rooms. It has now been restored and is in use as part of the theatre, the facade of the latter having been completely rebuilt. On the extreme right stand the St. Nicholas Almshouses, founded in 1652 and restored in 1961.

25. King Street was constructed in the seventeenth century and contained many gabled premises. The Llandoger Tavern, now known as the Llandoger Trow, was built in 1664 and stands on the corner of King Street and Queen Charlotte Street. Originally there was a projecting gable at the side, where the second chimney stack is situated, which was removed near the end of the nineteenth century. The word 'Trow' refers to a sailing barge which was owned by a Captain Hawkins. The barge travelled between Welsh Back, seen on the left of the illustration, to Llandoger, which is in the Wye Valley. The inn is linked with Daniel Defoe and Alexander Selkirk, and was certainly used by a number of privateers. Henry Irving patronised it, during his appearances at the nearby Theatre Royal. The two furthest gabled properties were destroyed in November 1940, as was the warehouse across the river. The street outside the inn has now been pedestrianised.

Christmas Street, and St. John's Arch, Bristol.

26. About 1907. Christmas Street looking from Rupert Street towards St. John's Arch into Broad Street. The street ran from Broad Street across Rupert Street and Narrow Lewins Mead to the bottom of Christmas Steps. The latter had once been a steep slope where in 1669 a vintner, Jonathan Blackwell, erected the steps at his own expense. St. John's Church above the arch is one of the smallest in Bristol; its tower stands on an archway which contained a city gate. The two arches for pedestrians were formed in the nineteenth century on either side of the gate. The properties on the right were demolished in 1931 for Electricity House; those on the left have also been removed, the site being redeveloped with a block incorporating the new magistrates' courts.

27. 1921. The corner of Rupert Street and Quay Street. Rupert Street was partially created in July 1857 by covering over the river Froom from the then St. John's Bridge to the Quay Head. The remaining section from the bridge back to Bridewell was covered in 1867. The figurehead of an Indian came from the S.S. 'Demerara', the largest steamship then built apart from the 'Great Britain'. The vessel was towed from Cumberland Basin on 10th November 1851, but following delays, the tide had turned before the ship passed the most dangerous parts of the Avon. Although badly damaged and initially thought of as a wreck, she was removed back to the entrance of Cumberland Basin. The building behind the statue was demolished for the erection of Electricity House. An attempt to remove the figure was made on 10th February 1931, but it fell to pieces.

AEROFILMS COPYRIGHT   GENERAL VIEW OF CENTRAL BRISTOL

28. The aerial view of Bristol taken about 1930 shows St. Augustines Parade and Broad Quay prior to the final works of culverting the Froom which were completed in 1940. On the right are the Co-operative Wholesale Society's premises, now rebuilt as offices, whilst behind them in Prince Street, a modern office block and the Unicorn Hotel have yet to be constructed along Narrow Quay. Dublin Shed, removed in 1937, can be seen standing opposite the buildings now occupied by the 'Bristol and West' tower block. Further to the right Prince Street roundabout has not been created and Queen Square has yet to be bisected by Redcliffe Way. On the left side of the Floating Harbour new sheds, now used for the Exhibition Centre, are under construction; the church of St. Augustine the Less still stands by the now void Royal Hotel, and the trees on College Green await removal.

VIEW OF BRISTOL'S DOCKS FROM THE AIR.

20

29. This aerial view of part of the Floating Harbour shows the layout of Queen Square just as it looked on Donne's Map of Bristol of 1826, a pleasant park surrounded by trees. Ordinarily, apart from Temperance processions and a few political meetings, the Square was a peaceful oasis in the heart of the City until bisected by Redcliffe Way in the 1930's. To the north the facade of Coopers' Hall stands out on the King Street frontage, and the edge of Bridge Street can be seen to the left of Bristol Bridge. Many of the buildings on the right bank around Redcliffe Street and Thomas Street were destroyed in the Blitz, as was Bridge Street and some of Baldwin Street. To the right of Bristol Bridge the new Robinson Building now occupies the site with the dome and a new office block is being built on the water's edge.

KING WILLIAM IV STATUE and DOCKS OFFICES, QUEENS SQUARE, BRISTOL.

30. Although the caption to this particular postcard refers to King William IV, it is in fact King William III. The statue, reputed to be the finest equestrian example in Europe, was erected in 1736 and is by Michael Rysbrack, a native of Antwerp. He came to London in 1720 and soon established himself as a leader in his profession. It should be noted however that the effigy lacks stirrups. When Redcliffe Way was built the ornate lamps and railings were removed. The row railings and seat in the foreground have also disappeared. Although the statue is seen here sideways on to the Docks Offices in the background, it was subsequently moved 45 degrees towards the camera so as to align with the new road.

View of Docks
Bristol.

No.3639.

Hayward Series

31. Even though the increasing size of vessels necessitated the provision of improved berthing facilities at the mouth of the Avon, this view of the western end of the floating harbour taken about 1912 shows the City Docks bustling with activity. On the right the timber yards of Baltic, Gefle, and Canada Wharves are packed with supplies. The site is now completely cleared awaiting a housing development. Looking to the left over the houses in Smeaton Road and Cumberland Road, the railway no longer runs along Merchants Dock and Hotwell Road, and a new residential development, Rownham Mead, comes down to the waterfront close to the first ship. Although no longer in use as a port, the City Docks are not dead; yachting, windsurfing, power boat racing and events such as the World Wine Fair have brought life back into this inner city area.

St. James' Barton, Bristol. 16

32. St. James Barton about 1906. The internationally important St. James Fair was held in this area from the Middle Ages. A gradual decline during the eighteenth century led to its abolition in September 1837. Afterwards a dispute over the ownership of the railed-in space took thirty years to resolve. Finally the City Council bought the ground for £8,000 and laid it out as a public park. St. James Church on the left was once a Benedictine Priory, and to the right of the tower there was a monastic building. The latter was demolished in the Reformation and the Parochial nave survived as the church. John Wesley's children were buried in the churchyard. An office block now stands between the two churches; all buildings to the right of the spire are now redeveloped with shops and offices and the spire removed. The quiet road to Bond Street is part of a busy dual carriageway.

Flower Market, Bristol.

33. About 1906. The flower market, looking through the arched entrance in High Street, across to the end of St. Mary-Le-Port Street. Before the building of markets there was a long-standing problem caused by people buying and selling produce in narrow streets. The erection of a market in 1745 between High Street and St. Nicholas Street was accompanied by an appropriate byelaw prohibiting buying and selling in the main streets. The Exchange and St. Nicholas markets were re-opened after reconstruction on 14th April 1849. At the time this view was taken flour was 4d. for 7 lbs, bedding plants were 1d. and 2d. each and a standard rose bush cost one shilling. Everything visible through the arch was blitzed in the Second World War.

34. Looking from Bristol Bridge along High Street, towards the spire of Christ Church (City). In the distance on the right is the Old Dutch House showing the renovations completed in 1909. With the exception of the tobacconists shop in the middle distance, everything on the right hand side of High Street has now disappeared. St. Mary-le-Port Street and Bridge Street, the junction of the latter is behind the policeman, were destroyed in the same air-raids. On the left of the picture the statue of Samuel Morley, a traffic hazard of the time until removed, stands in front of St. Nicholas Church. The latter is now a museum having been badly damaged in November 1940. On the church wall at the corner of High Street can be seen the Angel fountain. Originally erected in November 1859 it was removed for safety in 1941/42 and never replaced. Immediately behind the church new offices have been built on the corner of St. Nicholas Street.

35. Bristol Bridge about 1911. A bridge has existed near the site since the twelfth century. In 1768 a new structure was built, at a cost of £49,000, to deal with the traffic congestion. This was subsequently widened in two stages: first in 1861 the eastern parapet and two tollhouses were removed and a new footway constructed on iron cantilevers, then in 1873 the western parapet and two tollhouses were removed for the same purpose. The statue of Samuel Morley MP. (died in 1886) was unveiled on 27th October 1887 and subsequently moved to the Horsefair in 1921. Most of the buildings which can be seen were blitzed in the war. On 20th November 1893 the first permanent public electric lamps in the City were lit on Bristol Bridge.

Baldwin St., Bristol.

36. At its eastern end Baldwin Street follows a line taken by the old outer ditch of the City. It used to continue along what is now St. Stephen's Street, until in 1881 a new thoroughfare was cut from the lower end of Clare Street, including widening of the section of Baldwin Street nearest the camera. The purchase of properties, including a slice out of Marsh Street, cost £120,000 part of which was recouped from the sale of sites along the new frontages. For a while the new section was called New Baldwin Street. The properties to the left on the corner of Queen Charlotte Street were blitzed, and subsequently rebuilt in 1956. In the early morning, carts and barrows were brought into the street to take fruit and fish from the nearby markets to shops and householders. The wholesale market has since moved to St. Philips.

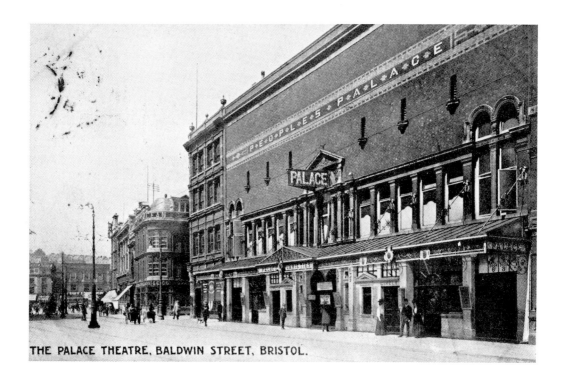

THE PALACE THEATRE, BALDWIN STREET, BRISTOL.

37. The People's Palace of Varieties in Baldwin Street opened on Boxing Day 1892 as a temperance Music Hall. The owners were the Livermore Brothers whose intention was 'to erect a really fine and artistic building... (as) a first rate Music Hall'. The designer was James Hutton; a number of halls were built throughout the country in the same style. The Palace could accommodate three thousand people and the high standard of entertainment that was provided, plus the electric lighting which was something of a novelty when it was installed, ensured its success. The manager, Mr. Charles Gascoigne, was a keen cinephotographer and his films of local events provided a welcome addition to the programme. Moving pictures gained ground as popular entertainment and the Palace became the Gaumont Cinema; the building is now a club. The ornate canopy has gone, and the facade is considerably altered at ground level.

General Post Office. Bristol.

38. The General Post Office in Small Street about 1906. As early as 1532 there is a record of someone being employed to carry a letter from Bristol to London. The Dolphin Inn in Dolphin Street was used as a post office prior to the erection of a building in All Saints Lane (removed in 1742 when the Exchange was built). This was followed by the use of a house in Small Street, then the post office moved to Exchange Avenue where the incised lettering can still be seen. The final transfer back to Small Street took place in 1868, where at first only the ground floor was used for postal business. The adoption of the halfpenny post for a variety of items, especially the postcard, brought a tremendous increase in postal business, some 93 million items being posted in Bristol in 1905. Six deliveries of letters, five deliveries of parcels and twelve collections were made daily at the time this picture was taken. The upper floors of the building were severely damaged on 6th December 1940 in an air-raid.

39. The Old Dutch House stood at the corner of High Street and Wine Street from 1676 to 1940. It was used for a variety of purposes, residential, a bank, then finally a shop. The question of its demolition or preservation was debated a number of times by the City Council, the main argument for its removal being proposals to widen the road. Finally in 1908 the Council decided by a majority of one to renovate the building. The balcony at roof level was removed and the shop was cut back to enable the pavement to be enlarged. Slender columns were utilised to support the upper storeys. The work was carried out in 1909 and the illustration shows the Dutch House prior to the renovations being undertaken. The building was gutted on 24th November 1940 and subsequently demolished by the military authorities. A dual carriageway was built over the site.

Old Dutch House, High Street, Bristol.

WINE STREET LOOKING EAST. BRISTOL.

40. Wine Street looking from Corn Street towards Narrow Wine Street. The turning to the left by Hope Brothers is the Pithay. A pillory once stood at this junction and it is possible that 'Wine' is a corruption of 'Wynch', a winch being on the pillory. One side of the street was almost monopolised by women's wear and household linens, with men's wear, jewellers, chemists and some of Bristol's chief restaurants found on the other side. Most of the big stores of the day had premises there which made it one of the City's major shopping thoroughfares. On the night of 24th November 1940 the entire area was destroyed in an air-raid and the buildings were cleared for new offices on the left-hand side, banks and a park on the right. The roadway was widened in the process.

BROADMEAD, BRISTOL.

41. Broadmead about 1908. A busy coaching centre in the nineteenth century; badly affected by flooding in March 1889. In 1811 John Breillat, a dyer at No. 56, experimented with illumination from coal gas. His shop and the street were lit in this way a year before any London street was so lit. On the right on the corner of Union Street are the premises of J.S. Fry and Sons which were gradually built up around the nucleus of a shop in Union Street. The Odeon Cinema now stands on the site. On the left is the junction of Lower Union Street with Strode, Cosh and Penfold the Chemists on the far corner. The tower of Broadmead Baptist Chapel rises up behind. The Greyhound Hotel on the right (middle to far distance) is the only building which still survives. Rosemary Street in the far distance has disappeared in the post-war rebuilding.

Lower Union St., Bristol. 2625.   York Series.

42. Lower Union Street about 1920. Looking through to the Horsefair the three storey buildings have given way to an office block. On the left-hand side Chamberlain, Pole and Company, corn and flour merchants, occupy No's 39 to 45 prior to the arrival of James Phillips and Sons who were then in No's 47 to 51. Strode Cosh and Penfold, chemists, occupy the opposite corner with Broadmead. Most of the street frontage is taken up by the Broadmead Baptist Chapel. The original building was constructed in 1671, then rebuilt in 1690. Considerable alterations and extensions were undertaken during the next two centuries. There was another entrance to the chapel from Broadmead itself. The spire is that of the Congregational Church and was demolished in 1956. The chemist's shop was rebuilt in 1954; Broadmead Chapel was rebuilt in 1969 with a row of shop fronts at ground level. There are now bank premises where the shop blinds are out in the background to the right.

Castle St Bristol. 62.

43. Castle Street was first laid out following the purchase (1630) and demolition (1655) of the Norman Castle, and was built upon the inner ward of the castle. The view illustrated was taken about 1913 looking towards Old Market from Peter Street. Next to Hayman's furnishing stores (No. 66) is the Cinema Theatre Picture Hall which closed in 1927. Beyond is Enoch Brownjohn's glass and china warehouse, and then the store of F.W. Woolworth and Company on the corner of Queen Street. Fisher and Sons umbrella stores are on the left at No. 21; a good quality umbrella could be bought for £1 at this time, a walking stick for five shillings. Castle Street became Bristol's most popular shopping area with its mix of small shops and large stores which remained open until 11 pm on a Saturday. The number of pedestrians prevented the use of the roadway by vehicles. The area was blitzed on 24th November 1940, and the shopping area rebuilt in Broadmead. Castle Street is now part of a large park.

Old Market S! Bristol. 53.

44. Castle Street, narrow and thronged with shoppers, opened out into what was Bristol's widest thoroughfare, Old Market, seen here as it was about 1913. On the left is the block of property that lay between the junction with Lower Castle Street and Careys Lane, just beyond the Empire Theatre. The Stag and Hounds Hotel where the Pie Poudre court was held can be seen in the distance, behind the oncoming motor-bus; it now forms the boundary of Old Market alongside an underpass which cuts across from left to right. All properties on the right from the hotel back towards the camera have been removed. The first electric trams in Bristol left from Old Market on 14th October 1895. It was remarked at the time that the ornamental poles showed up the poor design of the telegraph poles; also it is thought that the centre poles running up the length of Old Market were the first of their type used in this country. A modern hotel has been built on the left, and a pedestrian footbridge spans the underpass where the Empire Theatre once stood.

Old Market St., Bristol.

45. Old Market Street looking from West Street back over the City when the skyline was still dominated by church spires. The year is probably 1924 and the Central Hall is virtually completed. In 1923 the Old Market Street Chapel was demolished and the human remains which were in the burial ground were transferred to Greenbank Cemetery. A new methodist hall was constructed on the site plus the land made available by the purchase and demolition of four adjoining properties. The stonelaying ceremony was held on 23rd April 1923 and the new hall was opened on 29th April 1924 by the Reverend Dr. T. Ferrier Hulme, M.A., President of the Wesleyan Methodist Conference and former Chairman of the Bristol District Missionary. To the left of the Central Hall the first three buildings only remain; from there onwards all buildings were removed for an underpass and a hotel. In the distance on the left, a new office block has been built.

HOLYTRINITY BRISTOL.

46. Holy Trinity Church at the junction of Trinity Road and Clarence Road. Looking from West Street can be seen the twin towers of this Gothic style building designed by Thomas Rickman and Henry Hutchinson. Built in 1829, with later additions by J. Bevan Senior, the church is now redundant and used for community purposes. Its ornate railings disappeared in the Second World War and the gates have recently been removed. The cabman's rest in the middle of the road was erected in 1876; a cab can be seen waiting behind the policeman. Hiring of cabs was by distance or journey time, but unless otherwise agreed the hire was deemed to be by distance. Fares in 1905 were one shilling for the first mile or part of a mile, and sixpence for each subsequent half mile or part thereof. For timed journeys it was two shillings and sixpence for the first hour and sixpence for each subsequent quarter hour. From midnight to 6 am the rate was fare and a half. The building on the left is the old Trinity Road police station, since rebuilt.

VICTORIA ST. and NEPTUNE STATUE, BRISTOL

47. The coming of the steam train and the building of Temple Meads station considerably increased the flow of traffic in the roads leading from the latter into the City. Whichever way was chosen resulted in a tortuous route through narrow congested streets over a then much narrower Bristol Bridge. Ever conscious of cost and the pressure of those rate-payers who had the vote, the City Council hesitated to implement proposals for a more direct route, finally agreeing to lay out Victoria Street in 1871. Some £50,000 was spent clearing old property by cutting through Thomas Street and across Temple Street. Commercial premises were erected along the new frontage. Air-raids removed most of the buildings along Victoria Street and the warehouses have subsequently been replaced with commercial and wholesale premises.

Statue of
Neptune
Victoria St. Bristol
Fred Little. 191

48. Since 1949 Bristolians have become accustomed to the sight of Neptune's Statue standing on the City Centre with its back to the Floating Harbour. The first written mention of the statue seems to have been on 27th January 1728 in Farley's 'Bristol Newspaper'. It may well have been in existance as early as 1723 when the statue stood in the middle of Temple Street. It was then moved to Bear Lane, moved again in 1823 to Church Lane to make way for an extension to the then Dr. White's Almshouses, and finally moved to the junction of Victoria Street and Temple Street in 1872. The drinking fountain and pedestal illustrated were provided as a result of this last move; on the pedestal appeared a misleading inscription about the Armada. The drinking fountain did not survive the move to the City Centre; in 1983 it was necessary to carry out extensive repairs to the lead-covered figure.

49. St. Mary Redcliffe as seen from The Grove about 1906. The present building dates from about 1180 and covers three centuries of construction. This church has associations with John Cabot, discoverer of Newfoundland, William Penn, after whom Pennsylvania was named, Thomas Chatterton, the romantic boy poet, and George Frederick Handel, the composer. The Spire, struck by lightning in 1446, was rebuilt in 1872. Of cathedral-like proportions it is one of the largest and most beautiful English parish churches. A plumber, William Watts, invented the tower method of making lead shot following an inspired dream and built the tower to the right of the chimney onto his house (1698) in 1782. The castellated battlement had been added to remind him of Westminster Abbey! He made a fortune of £10,000 and lost it all in building speculation. The shot tower was demolished in 1968 and a new one constructed elsewhere in the city. To the left of the picture is the cone of a kiln used for glass manufacturing.

50. One hundred and fifty years have passed since a public meeting was held in the Guildhall, Bristol for the purpose of constructing a railway to London. The original Great Western railway station was built to the left of the picture in 1839-1841. The Great Western, the Bristol and Exeter and the Midland Railway Companies agreed to build Temple Meads as a joint station on the site of the old Bristol and Exeter Station. The buildings shown were erected between 1871 and 1878, the architect being Sir Matthew Digby Wyatt. Although the Parliamentary Bill enabling the work to be undertaken was introduced in 1865 the start was delayed by arguments over the proportion of costs to be borne by each company. The famous 'Blue Taxis' wait outside the station, beneath a clock tower, the roof of which has been destroyed.

Interior of Temple Mead Station. Bristol. (1)

51. The interior of Temple Meads Station looking out towards the north-eastern end. The general plan of the station was in the form of a 'V'. Through traffic passed along one side and Midland railway departures and local Great Western railway traffic started from the other. The volume of traffic into the station grew considerably towards the end of the nineteenth century and steps were taken to enable trains to and from South Wales to the West Country and London to avoid the station altogether. Platform No. 2 in the centre of the illustration has been removed, and so has No. 3 to its left. The four platforms were connected by a footbridge (also demolished) from which the photograph was taken. Extensive alterations were made to the station in the 1930's and the various platforms are now accessible only by means of subways.

52. The Royal Sovereign Temperance Hotel was situated at numbers 217/219 Clarence Road. From the middle ages Bristol has been a major wine importer and can boast of being one of the wine capitals of the world. However, drinking and the social evils that accompanied it became a great social problem and the Temperance Movement became very strong in Bristol, a number of different Temperance Associations being formed from the 1830's onwards. At first the movement was non-conformist, but was later taken up by the Church of England. It was recognised that alternative establishments had to be provided to counteract the 'evils' of the licensed houses and the music halls. Evangelical teetotalism was preached and for the non-drinking businessman there were Temperance hotels. A branch of the National Commercial Temperance League was founded in 1902 for businessmen who signed the pledge. The buildings in Clarence Road were demolished in 1959.

The Horsefair Bristol.

53. The Horsefair looking towards Bond Street and St. James Barton. Samuel Morley's statue, sculpted by J. Havard Thomas, had been moved from Baldwin Street in October 1921 and placed on an existing traffic island. It was moved again in 1971 to facilitate road improvements and has since been resited in a new position looking towards Union Street. St. James's Church on the left was built in 1130, a tower being added in 1374. The eastern end of the church was demolished in the Reformation. A modern office block has been built between St. James's and the adjoining Congregational Church, the spire of which was removed in 1956. The road is now a dual carriage way, John Lewis store stands on the extreme right and the shops and houses in the distance have been replaced with high-rise office blocks, a large traffic roundabout and a pedestrian underpass.

North St. Bristol.

54. North Street looking towards Stokes Croft in the middle distance, as seen from St. James Barton about 1910. Stead and Simpson's Boot Market occupies No. 9 on the left, with Bendalls Stores situated where the lady in white is standing. On the right-hand side on the corner of Moon Street is the 'Full Moon' Hotel which has existed in some form at or near this site as far back as the thirteenth century. It was mentioned in the Bristol Guide of 1825 as being one of the 'many excellent and accommodating Inns and Taverns in the City'. The building on the right below the advertisement for the luncheon bar has been replaced by a single story annexe to the hotel. The 'Full Moon' is the only building still in existance in this view of North Street. The road has been widened and is straddled by an office block.

Stokes Croft, Bristol

55. A view of Stokes Croft looking from North Street towards Cheltenham Road about 1906. Mickleburgh's piano store is on the left at the junction with King Square Avenue. In 1900 a Bechstein grand piano cost £210; an upright concert grand £105. A superior French violin could be bought for £2.50. On the right behind the sign for Meads Bazaar stood the Unitarian Almshouses and School. The alsmhouses were founded in 1726; the school was founded in 1722 by worshippers in the Lewins Mead Chapel. Initially the boys wore a uniform similar to that worn today by the boys of Queen Elizabeth's Hospital. Standing in the road on the left are two wheeled advertisement hoardings which were pushed around the streets. Most of the buildings which can be seen were lost in air-raids on 24th/25th November 1940. The frontages were rebuilt in the 1950's.

56. Stokes Croft at the junction with City Road and Upper York Street about 1912. Behind the workman and handcart on the right is City Road Baptist Chapel opened on 11th September 1861. Building costs, including a hall, were £5,500. The chapel could seat 900 persons who previously worshipped in the Pithay Chapel which was converted for use as part of the Fry's Factory complex. Tram No. 132 which is proceeding along City Road was introduced into service in 1897/98 and is one of a batch of low height types which were constructed so as to be able to negotiate the Eastville Park railway bridge on the Fishponds and Staple Hill route. No's 50 and 52 Stokes Croft, C.H. Clement the tailor, were demolished for road improvements in 1972. In the distance, to the right of the furthest tram, is the Baptist College which was demolished in the same year.

57. In the early hours of 27th March 1906 the alarm was received at the central police station, that Derham Brothers boot factory was on fire. The premises fronted onto Barton Street, Stokes Croft, and were well alight by the time the fire engines arrived. Wind blew the flames across the road engulfing the houses opposite, the occupants escaping with only the clothes they stood up in. The roar of the fire was heard as far away as the Prince's Theatre in Park Row where sparks landed in the roadway. The whole of Derhams, two houses on either side, the dwellings opposite and the cottages in Barton Court were destroyed. Part of the factory facade suddenly collapsed burying five firemen, one of whom, Arthur Wale, was killed. Office development now covers the site of the factory, north of Avon House North.

Funeral of Fireman Wale, March 30th. 1906.

58. The funeral of fireman Wale, victim of the Derham factory fire, was held on 30th March 1906. The funeral cortege left Bedminster police station at 2.50 pm and is seen here crossing Bedminster Bridge. The service was held at St. Mary Redcliffe followed by burial in Redcliffe Cemetery at Arnos Vale. Three mounted police led the mourners, followed by a detachment of police and the band of the 3rd Volunteer Battalion of the Gloucester Regiment. Three hundred constables including the chief constable and his deputy walked behind the three carriages of family mourners. Fireman Wale left a widow and ten children, and died only a month or so before completing the twenty-five years service which would have entitled him to a pension. A public appeal raised £602 in four days for his dependants and the sixty-two people made homeless by the fire.

59. The junction of Arley Hill and Cheltenham Road about 1907. The foundation stone of the former Congregational Chapel was laid on 22nd May 1845. Although the small island on which the lamp standard is situated remains to this day, the horse trough, lamp and the ornate railings around the chapel have been removed. The chapel itself is now in use as a Polish Catholic Church and a small outbuilding has recently been attached on the right-hand side. The houses have lost their covering of ivy and the first pair on the Cheltenham Road frontage open straight onto the pavement following the removal of the front walls and gardens. The shops at the Bath Buildings junction on the right have been demolished and a petrol filling station built on the site.

Free Library, Cheltenham Rd., Bristol.   No. 570.

60. The library on the corner of Winsley Road/Cheltenham Road about 1906. In 1850 Parliament authorised large towns to provide free public libraries. The maximum amount that a local authority could spend on such provision was the product of a 1d rate, a restriction that lasted until 1905. Bristol did not adopt the Public Libraries Act until 1874 and the Libraries Committee was only prepared to levy a ½d rate. To save money, existing buildings were adapted. North Bristol was served by a library situated in a large house in King Square, opened on 24th March 1877. The popularity of lending libraries amongst all classes of people and the evidence of demand for books on 'serious' subjects helped clear any lingering doubts about the propriety of spending rates for this purpose. The Cheltenham Road library was opened on 13th February 1901 by the Lord Mayor Alderman J. Godwin. It was destroyed in the Second World War and has since been replaced by a single story building.

General Hospital, Bristol.

61. The General Hospital in Bristol as seen about 1900. The original hospital had been founded in 1832 and paid for by public subscription. At that time anaesthetic had not been discovered and antiseptics were unknown. After 1850 the decision to treat persons living outside Bristol contributed towards a rapid increase in the number of patients. It was decided to build a new hospital and on 3rd August 1858 patients were transferred to the Italian style blue lias stone building erected in Guinea Street near the Bathurst Basin. At first there was great difficulty in obtaining women of suitable character to act as nurses and as late as 1864 nurses returning from leave were searched for alcohol before being allowed back on duty. The warehouses at ground floor level were let to augment the hospital's income. In 1912 a new southern wing by the architects Oatley and Lawrence, was added over the terraced area on the right of the picture. The dome was damaged in the Second World War and has been removed.

General Hospital, Bristol, (Proctor Baker Ward.)

62. The interior of the General Hospital, Bristol, about 1900. When the new General Hospital buildings opened in 1858 there were five wards for males and five for females each capable of taking sixteen beds. At a public meeting held on 6th May 1858 it had been decided that several of the wards should be named after persons who had contributed at least £1,000 towards the funding of the hospital. William Proctor Baker, a long-serving member of the City Council, was president of the General Hospital from 1872 until his death in 1907. He was instrumental in the replacement of the unhygienic cement floors with wooden ones. The National Health Insurance Act was not passed until 1910 and workers paid voluntary contributions as a means of insuring against the need for hospital treatment. Anaesthetics were introduced in 1847 (used for the first time in Bristol in 1850 at the Royal Infirmary), and antiseptics were used from the 1870's onwards.

OFF FOR A CRUISE
P.S. CAMBRIA BRISTOL

63. The Paddle Steamer 'Cambria' heading down river having passed under the Clifton Suspension Bridge; in the background the Portway has yet to be built. In 1887 a group of local businessmen chartered the paddle steamer 'Waverley' for work in the Bristol Channel. The success of this initiative led P. and A. Campbell to examine Bristol's potential as a station for their operations. 1888 was financially a poor year for the Company but 'Waverley' returned in 1889 and the Bristol public appreciated the speed, reliability and comfort the boat offered them. Campbells ordered additional steamers as business expanded, the 'Cambria's' trial trip on the Clyde being held on 24th May 1895. When built the 'Cambria's' saloon windows were square; here she is seen with the round ports fitted after the saloon windows were damaged in a gale in August 1908. After war service from 1939 to 1943 she was broken up having been damaged by fire in 1946.

Hotwell Rd., Bristol. 737.

64. Hotwell Road about 1906. The Hotwell, mention of which goes back as far as 1480, emerged at low tide from near St. Vincent's Rock and gave its name to this part of the City. The section of Hotwell Road illustrated runs west from Hotwells Baptist Chapel on the right, towards the junction of Merchants Road and Clifton Vale (behind the workman who is pushing the cart). The Hotwell tramway was electrified in 1899, the work being carried out in the winter in order to avoid the heavy summer traffic when passengers headed for the steamer and railway termini. The tramway closed in 1938. The buildings on the left and right of the picture, with the exception of those in the far distance, have disappeared. The road is now much wider and there is a recently constructed housing development, Rownham Mead, on the left-hand side.

The Dædalus, Bristol

65. The Mardyke, a view taken prior to 1911 showing the training ship 'Daedalus' at the mooring posts. Following the establishment of the Royal Naval Reserve in 1860, the 'Daedalus' was moored in the Floating Harbour in June 1861 to serve as a drill ship for the Bristol Royal Naval Volunteers and the Naval Reserve. It was from the frigate 'Daedalus' that the sighting of a huge sea serpent was reported in the South Atlantic, a sketch of the incident being printed in the Illustrated London News. The ship was towed down river and broken up in 1911. Behind the ship can be seen the Clifton Wood Industrial School which was established in 1849 as an alternative to imprisonment for young male offenders. The upper part of the school was previously the Clifton Workhouse, acquired by the school in 1859.

66. St. Georges Road Mens Club about 1904. The premises stood at No. 88 St. Georges Road and were the last of a rank of five buildings at the junction of Partition Street, to the right of the 'Three Tuns' public house. There were several clubs for workmen in the City in what were then described as the 'poor and thickly populated parishes'. The Adult School Movement had grown considerably in the first decade of the twentieth century, and having started on a religious basis soon recognised the need for recreational facilities. Billiards, skittles and quoits were just three of the interests catered for along with the reading rooms and refreshment facilities. The Movement was part of the Temperance and other socio-religious provision which flourished in the City up to the outbreak of the First World War. A garage and petrol filling station have since been built on the site.

The Lamb and Anchor, Milk St., Bristol.
"The Genuine Home Brewed House."

67. The 'Lamb and Anchor' stood at No's 32 and 34 Milk Street, on the corner with Leek Lane. Including hotels and ale and wine stores there were over thirteen hundred public houses in Bristol during the Edwardian period. The origin of the name 'Milk Street' is unknown but in view of other parts of the City having names incorporating 'cheese' and 'bread' the meaning may be straightforward. The proprietor of the public house at the time, G. Winstone, advertised it as 'The Genuine Home Brewed House'. In the days before the large breweries took over so many properties, brewing on the premises was not uncommon. Beer cost 6d per gallon, cider cost 14/- per dozen bottles and champagne was £5 per dozen bottles. Milk Street has disappeared in the post-war redevelopment of the Horsefair and Bond Street.

Copyright.

BRISTOL RUGBY FOOTBALL TEAM—Season 1904-5.

Bennett(Trnr.) H. Wellington(Sec.) Paul Chichester Vinnicombe Neads Davis J. W. Jarman(Chairman) G. E. Lockey
Watson Moore Thomas Smith(Vice-Capt.) Webb(Capt.) Lamond Shewring Meyer (Treas.)
Wood Oaten Spoors Oates

68. The Rugby Football Union was first formed in 1871. A year later the Clifton Rugby Club was founded and by 1905 it was playing three fifteens on a regular basis, its ground then being off Cranbrook Road West. The formation of the Bristol Rugby Club did not come about until 1888 when several of the clubs in the City amalgamated to form a representative side which played at the County Ground. There were some twenty other teams in existance in Bristol at the time, organised into four divisions by the Bristol and District Rugby Combination; there was also a local School's Union. Bristol was the second city in the country after Leicester to set up the latter form of organisation. Although not shown, J. Oates was also Honorary Secretary of the Club in 1905; Jarman, Moore and Shewring were England Internationals and Lamond played for Scotland. The Club did not move to the Memorial Ground until the 1921/22 season.

Bristol Tramways. Illuminated Car. December. 1925.

69. Each year between 1922 and 1927 a tramcar was decorated and used to collect money for the Lord Mayor of Bristol's appeal fund for children's Christmas dinners. The design for 1925 was Noah's Ark; it is seen here in the courtyard of Brislington Depot, which had a capacity of forty-eight cars and extensive workshop facilities. The decorated tram visited each part of the system and employees of the Company walked alongside it in fancy costumes collecting money. Because of the ease with which power was available large numbers of lights were included in the decorations. As much as £1,100 could be collected in a week from the large crowds who were attracted by the brightly illuminated car. Its place has been taken by an open top carol bus.

High Cross, College Green, Bristol.

188
PHOTO
HEPWORTH

70. College Green was once a fashionable residential area prior to the building of Queen Square. The erection of railings and the planting of the avenues of trees took place in the eighteenth century. The High Cross is not the original Civic High Cross. The latter stood at the junction of High Street/Corn Street and having been dismantled in 1733 was re-erected on College Green. It was removed in 1763 ostensibly because it stood in the way of the fashionable promenaders of the time. The foundation stone of a new High Cross was laid on 8th August 1850 by the Mayor, J.K. Haberfield, with full masonic rites. The cross was moved to the position shown in the picture in 1888 and a statue of Queen Victoria, which can be seen behind it to the right, was erected in its place. The outer row of trees was removed in 1927, the cross and inner row of trees removed in 1950, and the green lowered as part of the development of the new Council House which was opened on 17th April 1956.

71. In August 1740 Alderman Nathaniel Day was granted land to build an open street forty feet wide 'to lead from College Green up into the road towards Jacobs Well'. The area to be developed was known as Bullocks Park and twenty-two years after the original grant a start was made on what is now known as Park Street. Because of its width the street looks less steep than it really is; in 1856 consideration had been given to the installation of a cable car for drawing passengers and heavy loads up the hill. By 1866 approximately half of the fashionable houses had been converted to shops, a process completed by the 1880's. In November 1940 many of the shops were blitzed; the facades were rebuilt in the 1950's.

Princes Hotel, Park Row, Bristol. (adjoining Princes Theatre.)

72. Park Row showing the Prince's Theatre and the Prince's Hotel about 1906. The theatre was designed by C.J. Phipps, architect of a number of London theatres such as the Gaiety, the Lyric and His Majesty's. It opened on the 14th October 1867 having cost the proprietor, James Henry Chute, £20,000. The first performance was Shakespeare's 'The Tempest', which ran for a month, and the first pantomime was 'Aladdin'. Originally the theatre was called the New Theatre Royal, being renamed The Prince's in 1884. In 1869 during a Boxing Night performance of 'Robinson Crusoe' eighteen persons were trampled to death in an incident at the pit and gallery entrance. The shelter at the entrance was built in 1902 along with a new foyer and separate entrances and exits to all parts. The theatre became famous for its pantomime and George Bernard Shaw considered it the best in Europe. Hotel, theatre and buildings to the left were destroyed on 24th November 1940. A filling station and a block of flats now occupy the site.

73. Queens Road, looking across to the end of Park Row on the extreme right. The edge of the former City Museum, built in 1867, is on the left. The interior was gutted in the Second World War and it is now in use as the University Refectory. Beyond the Art Gallery is the headquarters of the Bristol Rifle Corps and next to it rises the Gothic structure of the School of Industry for the Blind which was first occupied in 1838. The aim of the school was to aid the adult blind of the City by teaching them a trade and then finding them suitable employment. The main trade was basket weaving; brushmaking, chair caning and machine knitting were also introduced. The Drill Hall and Asylum were acquired by the University and demolished in 1915. The University Tower and extensions stand on the site; the road is now a busy dual carriageway.

The Art Gallery Queen's Rd, Bristol.

74. Looking towards Queen's Road from the junction of Park Street and Park Row about 1910. A traffic island now lies where tram No. 11 is standing, and extends up towards the Queen's Road/Triangle junction in the distance. The Art Gallery on the right was opened by Professor Hubert Herkomer on 15th February 1905. It had been paid for by Sir W.H. Wills (later Lord Winterstoke) and cost £40,000. Tram No. 12 is standing beside the Headquarters of the Bristol Rifle Corps. The latter moved to a new drill hall in Old Market in 1915 and the old buildings were demolished in the same year, the site along with that of the Blind Asylum, seen behind the tree, was used for additions to the University, including the Tower, which were opened in 1925.

75. About 1906, Lennards Corner at the junction of Triangle West and Queen's Road, destroyed in an air-raid on 24th November 1940. Lennards, also known as the 'Public Benefit Boot Company', had their warehouse and headquarters in the Queen's Road premises. Their branches were spread throughout London, South Wales, and the West Country. The entrance to the retail premises was on the left of the picture. Messrs. Newbery's Ltd., house furnishers, occupied most of the remaining ground floor shops and Messrs. Cater, Stoffell and Fortt Ltd., grocers, wine and spirit merchants, were at No. 97, Queen's Road, to the rear of the horse and cart. New retail premises now occupy the entire site. Park Place is off to the right; the wall and hedge no longer exist.

Queen's Hotel, Clifton, Bristol, DAVID CROMBIE, *Managing Director.*

76. The Queen's Hotel Clifton, on the corner of Queen's Road and Queen's Avenue. The latter once led into a large park owned by the Tyndall family which lay around Royal Fort House and stretched almost to Whiteladies Gate. The Hotel was opened in 1854. In 1913 a table d'hote luncheon was available from 1 pm at a cost of 2/6 per head; table d'hote dinners were served daily from 7 pm at a cost of 3/6 per head. Car accumulators were charged free to hotel visitors. From 1914 to 1918 the hotel was used by the army. Subsequently it became a plumbers showroom and a retail store. The canopy over the side entrance has gone as has the walled area at the front which is now paved over. Large plate glass windows have replaced those shown at the ground floor level front and side. The buildings on the other side of Queen's Avenue where the taxis are standing have given way to a modern bank and offices.

Unveiling of the Memorial to the Heroes of the Gloucestershire Regiment by Field Marshal Lord Roberts, V. C., K. G., at Bristol, on March 4th. 1905.

Harvey Barton's Series

77. On Saturday 4th March 1905 Field Marshal Lord Roberts unveiled a memorial to the soldiers of the Gloucester Regiment who gave their lives in the Boer War. Lord Roberts was a Freeman of the City of Bristol who lived for many years in the suburbs. He won the Victoria Cross at Khodagunge during the Indian mutiny when he was a Lieutenant in the Bengal Artillery. The Gloucesters suffered heavy casualties at Nicholsons Nek during the siege of Ladysmith; subsequently they assisted at the relief of Kimberley under the overall command of Lord Roberts. Prior to the unveiling ceremony the Colours of the 2nd Battalian the Gloucester Regiment were handed back to them at the Council House. There was little decoration in the streets, where the Gloucester Regiment and the North Somerset Yeomanry lined the route. Lord Roberts arrived at Temple Meads and drove to the Victoria Rooms via the old Council House. He unveiled the bronze figure on its pedestal of granite, designed by Mr. Onslow Whiting of London, and then proceeded to the Mansion House for lunch with the Lord Mayor.

78. The Victoria Rooms, designed by the architect Charles Dyer. Work started in 1840 and the building was opened on 24th May 1842. There was accommodation for 1,700 people in the saloon; two other rooms were capable of seating 400 and 110 people respectively. The figure in the chariot above the columns represents the goddess Minerva. The Royal Agricultural Show of 1842 was the first public occasion on which the building was used. Inside the railings can be seen the pair of sphinx which were situated on either side of the front steps. These were removed, along with the railings and gates, in 1912 in order to build the fountains and the statue in memory of Edward VII. A grassed traffic island now surrounds the war memorial in the roadway.

79. The upper part of Whiteladies Road has long been known as Blackboy Hill, and a public house of that name stood near to the spot until 1874. Behind the tram on the left was the entrance to the Bristol Tramways and Carriage Company's Redland garage. Private touring cars or Blue Taxis could be hired, the former complete with 'reliable and experienced drivers in private livery'. The advertisement for the 'Triangle' refers to the Triangle Hill Picture House in Triangle West, Clifton, which was blitzed in the Second World War. Blackboy Hill was on the tram route to Westbury-on-Trym and Eastville; the tram service numbers and three lines of route detail which can be seen were a feature introduced on 14th November 1913. The advertising hoardings were removed in the early 1950's and a petrol filling station now occupies the site.

80. The top of Blackboy Hill about 1918. Upper Belgrave Road runs from left to right of the picture; it was the tram terminus for cars to Eastville and the Centre via Zetland Road. To the right of the tram is the Urijah Thomas Memorial drinking fountain erected in 1903. The Reverend U.R. Thomas was Minister of Redland Park Congregational Church for many years and was noted for his religious, educational and charitable activities. The First World War Tank was one of a number used throughout the country to advertise War Bonds and National Savings Certificates. The picture clearly illustrates the ornate beauty of everyday objects of the time such as tram poles and fences. On top of the right hand pole can be seen the 'Bristol' style wreath and spear finial which was manufactured by the Bromford Tube Company Ltd., Birmingham.

At the top of "Black Boy" Hill.

81. Before the tramway system was extended to Westbury village in 1908, a horse bus service operated from the top of Blackboy Hill with effect from December 1900, running between Westbury, Redland and Sneyd Park. On 27th October 1905 the Bristol Tramways and Carriage Company Ltd. undertook a trial run of a Thorneycroft bus chassis. It was considered a success and following the delivery of the first chassis on 1st December 1905; a service was opened between Redland and Westbury on 8th February 1906. The bus illustrated was fitted with an open staircase, the body being by the United Electric Car Company of Preston. It seated sixteen passengers inside, two at the front and nineteen on the open top.

WESTBURY RD.
DURDHAM DOWN BRISTOL.118.

82. About 1913. Westbury Road, Durdham Down, the 'white tree' to the left of the picture. Durdham Down, consisting of some 212 acres, was acquired with Clifton Down (230 acres) under the provisions of the Clifton and Durdham Downs Act of 1861, 'as places of recreation for ever'. Clifton Down was in the hands of the Society of Merchant Venturers who abandoned their rights for nothing. Durdham Down belonged to the Lords of the Manor of Henbury who received £15,000 in return for the surrender of rights. The Downs are some 300 feet above the level of the old City and have long been used for sports such as football, cricket and in earlier decades, hockey, lacrosse and golf. The area has retained much of its original character as a grassy plateau with numerous drives.

83. About 1908 Regent Street, Clifton looking down towards Clifton Hill. To the left is Merchants Road with the store of John Cordeux and Sons, general furnishers (replaced by 'Bobbys' in 1928) on the corner; to the right, is the junction of Royal York Crescent. The trams were never permitted to extend into the Clifton village area; instead a horsebus, subsequently a motorbus, conveyed passengers from the Victoria Rooms as far as the Suspension Bridge. This fashionable suburb with its beautiful views of the Avon Gorge, and its handsome Georgian terraces was once known as Clistone. There were two manors, one held by the College of Westbury, the other in lay hands. Although Clifton expanded during the heyday of Hotwells, it was in the early nineteenth century that it took on the role of a 'recuperative residential resort'. The buildings on the left were blitzed in 1941 and have since been replaced.

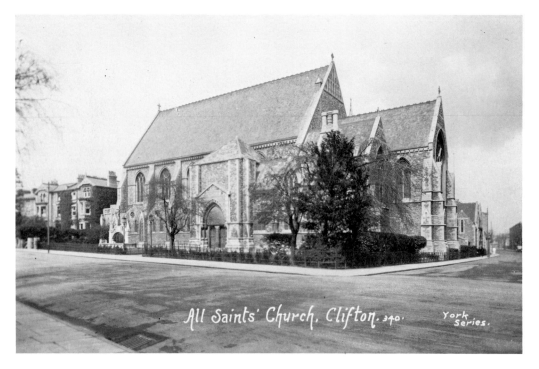

All Saints' Church, Clifton. 340. York Series.

84. All Saints Church, Clifton in the 1920's. The foundation stone was laid on 3rd November 1864 and the building was completed in 1868, the architect being George Edmund Street. A choir school was established in 1869. It was the first Anglo-Catholic Church to be built in Clifton, partly in response to the needs of people who otherwise had to travel to St. Raphael's Church in Bedminster. The church was supported by the local Society for Promoting Freedom of Public Worship which opposed the pew system that gave the wealthy and those who were non-residents in the parish the monopoly of the reserved seats. The design of the church allowed 1,000 people an unbroken view of the chancel, altar and pulpit. On Monday, 2nd December 1940 the building burnt out as the result of incendiaries from a German air-raid. Most of the valuable ornaments, plate and vestments were removed to safety before the roof collapsed. The parish hall was converted into a temporary church pending restoration work which was completed in 1967.

85. The Bristol, Clifton and West of England Zoological Society was formed by some two hundred and twenty Bristolians who each subscribed the sum of £25 per share. The original deed of trust laid down that subscribers should receive no dividend, but that any surplus revenue should be directed to improving the property. The Zoological Gardens were first opened to the public on 11th July 1836, and occupy a twelve acre site which was purchased from a Mr. F. Adams for £3,456. A further £5,300 was spent to provide suitable buildings and to lay out the gardens. The entire operation was masterminded by a Mr. Forrest of Acton, London. The north entrance to the zoo, situated on the Clifton Down frontage, is seen here complete with old turnstiles and vending machines. The gate houses have now been connected and form a continuous frontage.

The Swing at Clifton Zoo.

86. From its inception, the Bristol, Clifton and West of England Zoological Society found it difficult to generate sufficient income to cover its expenses. It had to find a middle way between being a scientific establishment and a commercial venture. The gardens were not open to the public on Sundays until the early 1920's, the only day when the working class could normally visit them, so fêtes and other activities were needed to produce revenue. Boat trips on the lake, tennis courts, and swings were some of the additional attractions for the paying customers. The swing shown was situated by the entrance gate in Guthrie Road, opposite Clifton College, a very useful source of revenue from 1862 onwards when parents wished to take their sons for an outing. The swing existed in the 1880's, but in common with the surrounding trees has been removed in the course of improvements to the gardens.

LADY WHITE'S STALL BRISTOL CARNIVAL

FRANK HOLMES PHOTO.

87. When Sir Charles Cave, the President of the Bristol Royal Infirmary, resigned in 1904 his place was taken by Sir George White, Bart. There was an outstanding debt of £15,500 in the hospital's account and strenuous efforts were taken by the new President to raise funds, both to clear the deficit and to provide for a much needed enlargement of the Infirmary. The Clifton Zoo was a popular venue for fund-raising events and a carnival was held there which opened on 26th June 1905 and lasted a whole week. The result was a profit of £7,500 which Sir George matched pound for pound from his own pocket. Lady White had her own stall along the main avenue in the zoo; apart from stalls and side shows, concerts were held in a large marquee fitted out with chandeliers and a stylish stage, and bands played in the open air on a gaily decorated rostrum.

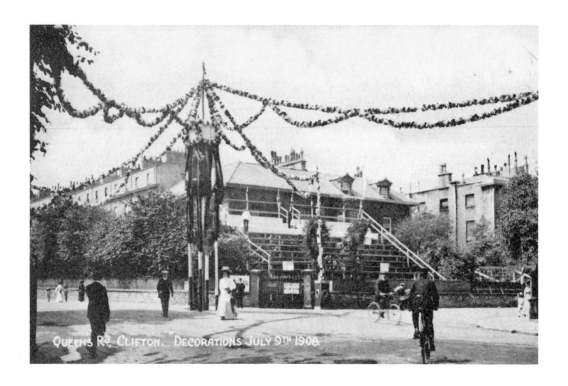

QUEENS Rᵈ, CLIFTON. DECORATIONS JULY 9ᵀᴴ 1908.

88. The decorations for the Royal Visit of 1908 were provided by both the City Council and a large number of private firms. The latter decorated and illuminated their premises and in some cases provided stands along the processional route from which the public could obtain an uninterrupted view of the proceedings. John Cordeux and Sons, who had a store in Merchants Road, Clifton, provided this stand on the corner of Queens Road and Pembroke Road and another in Upper Belgrave Road. The empty houses at the rear were available for lunches and teas. Tickets were issued which included a seat and a good luncheon. Ever mindful of revenue, the City Council levied a rate on each stand based on the cost of construction and one week in situ. Verrier and Company of Wine Street advertised special Royal Visit silk blouses from 4/11 to 25/-. The Chief Constable felt obliged to issue a warning against 'light fingered gentry on the route'.

Visit of S.M. the King & Queen to open the Royal Edward Dock, Avonmouth, July 9th 1908

89. As ships became larger it was obvious that the City Docks could not cope with them and rival docks began to spring up at Portishead and Avonmouth. These were acquired by the City Council and properly equipped and enlarged. However to remain at the forefront of docks operations even longer berths were required and in March 1902 the Prince of Wales (later King George V) dug the first sod of the proposed Royal Edward Dock. On completion of the work King Edward VII and Queen Alexandra performed the opening ceremony on 9th July 1908. The Royal procession made its way from Temple Meads to Clifton Down Station. The Royal carriage can be seen outside the Art Gallery on Queens Road where lunch was waiting. The line of elderly gentlemen are local veterans of the Crimean War who were given a place of honour on the occasion of Royal visits to the City.

The VICTORIA and ALBERT, with the KING on Board, breaks the Ribbon
at the entrance of the Dock, Avonmouth, July 9th 1908.
OUR SOVEREIGN SAID – "I Declare the Royal Edward Dock now open."

90. The Royal Yacht 'Victoria and Albert' anchored at the entrance of the Royal Edward dock to await the arrival of the Royal party on 8th July 1908. On the following day the King and Queen went by train from Avonmouth to Temple Meads Station. After a procession through the city they returned to Avonmouth by train from Clifton Down station. Having gone back on board the Royal Yacht the latter steered forward, breaking the ribbon placed across the dock entrance, and berthed alongside the east wharf. Accompanied by the Lord Mayor and the Bishop of Bristol the Royal Party mounted a dais and King Edward formally announced that '...the Royal Edward Dock (is) now open'. As part of the new dock two large transit sheds were provided on the eastern side and behind them a large granary. A new railway connection was laid down to Filton which reduced the distance between Avonmouth and London by 14 miles. Passengers could be in London within two hours of disembarking at the station.

91. The proclamation coach outside the Old Council House on the corner of Corn Street and Broad Street on 14th May 1910. Edward VII died on 6th May 1910 and an Order in Council was sent to the City Council instructing them to arrange the proclamation of King George V. The ancient ceremonial coach dates from at least 1801 and has been used since that time for great public occasions, including the proclamation of peace in 1801 and 1813. Although Queen Victoria was proclaimed from seven points in the City the latter were reduced to four in 1910; the cross-roads at the top of High Street, the Haymarket, College Green and Queen Square. The actual form of the proclamation was the same as that used in London, and was read by the sheriff, Mr. George Riseley. The arrangements were similar to those carried out for Edward VII on January 26th 1901, and attracted vast crowds of sightseers along the route and at the proclamation points.

The Royal Visit to Bristol.
Their Majesties Arrival at the Council House.

No. 16.

92. The Royal visit to Bristol on Friday 28th June 1912, was the first since the King's accession to the throne. Its main purpose was for the official opening of the King Edward VII Memorial Infirmary in Marlborough Street. On arrival from Cardiff by train, the Royal couple drove to the old Council House in Corn Street, arriving at 2.07 pm. A stand had been erected in front of the facade where the Aldermen and City Councillors were waiting and the Loyal Address was read by the Town Clerk Edmund J. Taylor. The King responded and then knighted the Lord Mayor Frank W. Wills, a son of the late Mr. H.O. Wills. Former Lord Mayors were presented to the King and Queen. At 2.19 pm the Royal carriage left for Canynge Road, Clifton. College Green which was on the processional route was deliberately left undecorated so that the natural setting of trees, High Cross and Cathedral could be admired by the King and Queen.

The Royal Visit to Bristol
Their Majesties Witnessing the Living Union Jack
formed by 2500 School Children

93. Apart from opening the new Infirmary buildings on 28th June 1912, King George V and Queen Mary undertook a number of minor engagements along the processional route. They arrived at Canynge Road at 2.46 pm, the Royal Escort being provided in front and behind their carriage by the North Somerset Yeomanry. In the playing field of Clifton College, 2,500 children had assembled, arranged in the formation of a living Union Jack. Each child wore the appropriate clothing to reproduce the flag's colours. The children were controlled by marshals and a man on a dais with a white flag who signalled when they were to kneel as the King and Queen entered the field. The display was a re-enactment of the Empire Day 'living flag', which was formed at the Ashton Gate football ground.

The Royal Agricultural Show. Bristol. 1913.

94. The Royal Agricultural Show of 1913. It was open from Tuesday, 1st July, until Saturday, 5th July and occupied a 100 acre site on the Downs. The implements and machinery in motion were situated behind the main entrance at the top of Blackboy Hill and along the Stoke Road frontage. The British Agricultural Society had been inaugurated in 1838 and received its Royal Charter in 1839. Agricultural shows were held annually by the Society, previous shows in Bristol being in 1842 (six acres at the rear of the Victoria Rooms with the ploughing competition at Beggars Bush and farm implement trials at Sneyd Park) and in 1878 (at Durdham Down on a site near to Westbury Road). Admission to the show was five shillings on the first day, two shillings and six pence on the second and third days and a shilling on the fourth and last days.

The Royal Agricultural Show. Bristol. 1913.

No. 6.

95. Tuesday, 1st July 1913. The first day of the Royal Agricultural Show. Judging of the cattle started at nine in the morning. The showyard was open to the public from eight in the morning until nine in the evening and there was a carriage drive surrounding it with access from the roads around the site. Cattle were shown in two large rings with a separate horse ring and grandstand. The manure yard was sited immediately behind the workmens' refreshment area. Total prizes offered at the show amounted to £11,000. There were 95 classes of horses and 126 classes of cattle, in addition to numerous classes of sheep, pigs and poultry. The first prize for the bulls being exhibited was £10. A contemporary advertisement in the exhibition catalogue offered a 200 acre farm in New Brunswick, Canada, equipped with horse and farm buildings, livestock and farm implements for the sum of £550.

Royal Show. 1913.
His Majesty Leaving the Victoria Rooms.

No. 24

96. Friday 4th July 1913. King George V leaves the Victoria Rooms where a statue of his father had been unveiled. The King, accompanied by a Lord-in-Waiting and two equerries, travelled from London to Temple Meads by special train arriving at 12 noon. His own carriage awaited him and he drove via Victoria Street, Baldwin Street, St. Augustines, College Green and Queens Road. He did not descend from his carriage on arrival at the Victoria Rooms where he received an address from the Lord Mayor. The statue was unveiled by the time he arrived. The King then went on to the Royal Show and was received by the Honorary Director of the Royal Agricultural Society, Sir Gilbert Greenall. He left the show grounds at 4.20 pm and the Royal Train left Temple Meads about 5.00 pm.

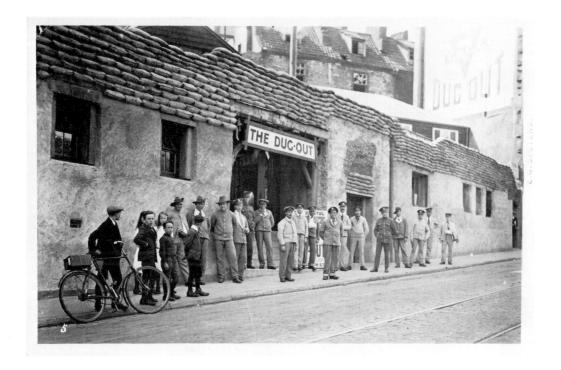

97. The YMCA Forces Canteen in Colston Street which was opened on 17th May 1917. Above the sandbagged frontage can be seen the derelict properties at the rear of Trenchard Street. These were subsequently improved and incorporated in the 'Dug Out' as the canteen was known. Wounded soldiers were often brought straight from the front line and were returned to England, arriving by special trains at stations such as Temple Meads for subsequent dispersal to one of the local war hospitals for treatment and recuperation. The 'Dug Out' had beds for 140 servicemen, with canteen and recreational facilities such as billiards. During the two years the canteen was open over one million servicemen were able to benefit from it.

98. Colston Avenue on the City Centre, 28th March 1915. At the time of the First World War, marches and demonstrations were used to encourage the patriotic spirit of the bystanders, prior to the introduction of conscription, and to draw attention to the example of organisations such as the Boys' Brigade from whose ranks some of the soldiers and servants of the Empire would come. The Brigade had been established locally in 1891 on non-sectarian lines with the object of promoting 'habits of reverence, discipline, self-respect and all that tends towards a true Christian manliness'; boys between the ages of 12 to 17 were eligible to join. All buildings on the right leading to Clare Street have been rebuilt. In the background Electricity House now stands and the wall and railings have disappeared following revisions to the road pattern.

Church Lads Brigd. 24/5/15 Empire Day. 776

99. A military recruitment parade was organised for Empire Day, 24th May 1915. It left Queen Square at 2.40 pm marching via St. Augustines Bridge, Park Street and Whiteladies Road to the Downs. Here it is seen passing the Bristol Academy of Fine Arts; in the background to the right can be seen 'Lennards Corner' blitzed in 1940. There were 5,000 persons taking part in the procession, 300 of whom were the 1st Cadet Battalion of the Church Lads Brigade. Behind them can be seen four motor vans of the British Red Cross. On arrival at the Downs there was a review by the General Officer Commanding (Southern Command) Lieutenant General Pitcairn Campbell. The Bristol Citizens Recruiting Committee had set up four platforms, one of them being under the Chairmanship of Sir George White Bart., who spoke to the large crowd about the need to support the war effort. A large number of young men subsequently volunteered to join the Armed Forces.

100. The Tramway Centre in 1915 looking along Colston Avenue towards Rupert Street. On the horizon to the right can be seen Fry's Factories situated around the Broadmead/Pithay area, prior to their move to Keynsham. To the left is the spire of St. John the Baptist, Broad Street. All the buildings behind the troops, to the left of the spire, were demolished for the erection of Electricity House. The buildings on the extreme left of the picture have been demolished for a new office block. The single story public toilets in the foreground were removed in the 1970's. Two companies of the Black Watch arrived in Bristol from Salisbury Plain on 10th November 1914. Rifle practice took place in the rifle range at the foot of the Sea Walls and there were charabanc trips to local beauty spots and places of interest. The troops left Bristol on 21st April 1915.

101. The British expedition to the Dardanelles in 1915 was organised in response to requests from Russia which needed some relief after heavy fighting in December 1914. The initial landing took place on 25th April 1915 and became bogged down into trench warfare, the Turks having been taken by surprise at first. General Sir Ian Hamilton was the commander-in-chief of the expeditionary force; he is seen here inspecting four hundred survivors of the campaign who mustered in Colston Avenue for the fourth anniversary of the Gallipoli landings which were celebrated on Saturday 26th April 1919. Behind Sir Ian is the Lord Mayor Alderman H.W. Twiggs, wearing the gold chain of office purchased by the City Council in 1828. The buildings behind the assembled men have since been demolished; in the background is Burke's statue and the public toilets, the latter also demolished. After the inspection there was a coach drive to the Old Council House in Clare Street where Sir Ian took the salute; he then drove to the Art Gallery for lunch, ending the day's programme with a visit to the Hippodrome.

Prince of Wales Visit to Bristol
10TH JUNE 1921.   A.G.S & Co.B.   No.3
Our Prince greets his Comrades,

102. Friday 10th June 1921 was a public holiday in the City for the visit of the Prince of Wales, later King Edward VIII. At 12.30 pm he was driven from the Colston Hall to Queen Square which had been reserved for ex-servicemen, cadets and scouts. Alighting opposite the Customs House, the Prince received a tumultuous welcome, and he proceeded to inspect those present, recognising some whom he had not seen for several years. The ability to recall a previous meeting was a particular feature of the Prince's character. The gentleman in naval uniform is Admiral Halsey, the Prince's Equerry. Prince Edward then walked up the main avenue to the statue of King William III where he made a speech in which he referred to the plight of some of the ex-servicemen, and expressed the hope for better times ahead. At 1.00 pm he went to Merchants' Hall for lunch, and was made an Honorary Freeman of the Society of Merchant Venturers.

ROYAL VISIT TO BRISTOL.
THE KING INSPECTING GUARD OF HONOUR AT TEMPLE MEADS.

No 1

103. On Tuesday 9th June 1925, King George V and Queen Mary came to Bristol to open the newly built extensions to the University (The Wills Memorial Building). It was the first visit to the City by both King and Queen since they held an investiture on the Downs on 8th November 1917. Having left Windsor Station at 10.00 am the Royal Train arrived at Temple Meads shortly after 12.00 noon. The King is seen here inspecting a Guard of Honour formed by the 4th and 6th Battalions of the Gloucester Regiment under Captain C.A.R. Beckett M.C. The King wore a morning coat with a white carnation, and a light grey silk hat. Standing immediately behind him is General Sir Alexander Godley K.C.B., K.C.M.G., the General Officer Commanding (Southern Command). During the inspection the Queen stood in the entrance to the station talking to the Duchess of Beaufort. On the left can be seen the Chief Constable J.H. Wilson O.B.E., standing by his white open-top car which headed the procession to the University Union at the Victoria Rooms where lunch was held. Ticket holders only were admitted to the station incline.

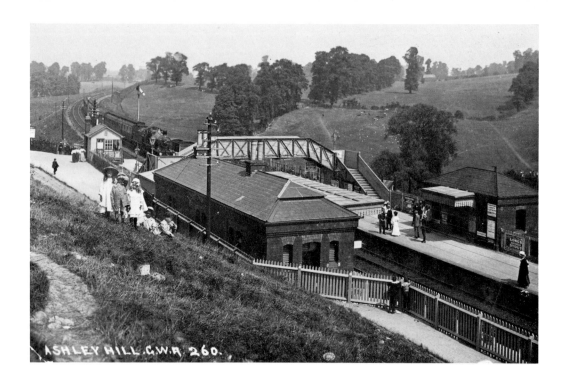

ASHLEY HILL. G.W.R. 260.

104. Ashley Hill Station about 1910. Built as part of the South Wales Link, Ashley Hill Station was opened on 13th August 1864. To the west of the railway line the Ashley Down area was already residentially developed at the time this picture was taken. On the other side of the track, green fields and allotments stretched as far as Eastville Park, broken only by farms and isolated houses. 'Ashley' is probably derived from the Manor of Asseley referred to in a charter dating from the twelfth century. A conduit which used to stand at the end of St. Stephens Street in the City Centre had its source at a point close to the railway station. The latter was closed to passengers on 23rd November 1964, and to goods services on 1st November 1966. The footbridge and station buildings have now been removed. Muller Road has been cut through the fields shown in the picture, which are now a mixture of allotment land and residential development.

105. George Muller opened his first home for orphans in 1836 in Wilson Street, Bristol. The number of children requiring assistance necessitated the purchase of further houses in the same street, and he decided to embark upon an ambitious scheme of purpose built accommodation at Ashley Down. Between 1849 and 1870 five orphanages for 2,050 children were built at a cost of £115,000. The picture shows a group of orphans sitting on the footbridge at Ashley Down Station. The footbridge was built in 1903 and has since been removed. A day's outing for the orphans in the Edwardian period often consisted of a walk from the orphan houses, across what is now Muller Road to Purdown where there were swings hanging from some of the trees. Muller always insisted that no one connected with his work had ever asked for money, but relied on faith alone for funding the building costs and day to day running expenses. The orphan houses are now occupied by Brunel Technical College.

Ashley Rd. & Grosvenor Rd. Bristol. 224.

106. Much of Bristol changed as a result of the effects of bombing raids in the Second World War. Other parts, especially those in the inner city areas, have been radically altered following decisions to remove existing houses en masse and replace them with either multistorey blocks (the fashion of the 1950's and 1960's), or more latterly mixed developments of low rise housing. A proposal to clear parts of the St. Paul's area and redevelop the sites was partially implemented at the junction of Ashley Road and Grosvenor Road. The buildings illustrated were gradually cleared in the early 1970's and the area extending to the flank wall with the advertisement in Ashley Road is now a grassed open space. Beyond it are new houses and flats built for the City Council. The buildings on the extreme left remain except for those in Grosvenor Road beyond the horses and carts.

107. The Bedminster Hippodrome stood in East Street in the block of properties between Essex Street and Lombard Street. A branch of Brooks Dye Works was at No. 60 East Street; the nearest buildings on the right were No's 38 and 40, the premises of Vessey and Abington, clothiers. The Hippodrome was opened on 7th August 1911, the proprietor being Walter De Frece. He was unable to obtain a licence for dramatic performances and although there were appearances such as the Beecham Opera Company in 1912, the theatre was not a success. In 1914 De Frece sold the building to Oswald Stoll who reopened it as a silent cinema in April 1915. On 5th January 1941 the Bedminster Hippodrome was bombed; the remains were demolished in 1954 for a store.

Zetland Road Junction, Bristol. 44

108. Zetland Road junction, Bishopston, as it appeared in the Edwardian period. The Wilts and Dorset Bank is newly completed and stands on the site formerly occupied by S.T. Pont, who supplied English and Italian provisions. Looking up the main Gloucester Road, the houses on the left have yet to lose their front gardens as increasing trade from suburban expansion justified their conversion to shops. On the opposite side of the road to the right of the wagon, the Prince of Wales public house has recently incorporated the shop with the blind into its premises. Far right behind the tram, was the Bishopston Branch of the Bristol Tramways and Carriage Company, since replaced by a furniture store. This area used to be subject to flooding from Cutlers Mill Brook in what is now Cranbrook Road.

THE WHITE HART HILL, BRISLINGTON. SLTN. 3

Copyright Lilywhite
Sowerby Bridge.

109. About 1908. The village of Brislington did not form part of the City of Bristol until the boundary extensions of 1933, although the area known as 'New Brislington' lay within Bristol after the boundary extension of 1897. The tram terminus was just behind where the photographer took this picture. The White Hart Hotel on the right still survives, without its porch, but Linden Farm beyond it was demolished some time after 1924 for residential development. During its existance the farm supplied milk to most of the surrounding area. The wall on the left of the road formed the boundary of Brislington Hill House. Wall and house have been demolished and a block of flats, shops and a broad highway have been built on the site. At the time this picture was taken the hotel and farm buildings marked the limit of residential development in the south-east of Bristol.

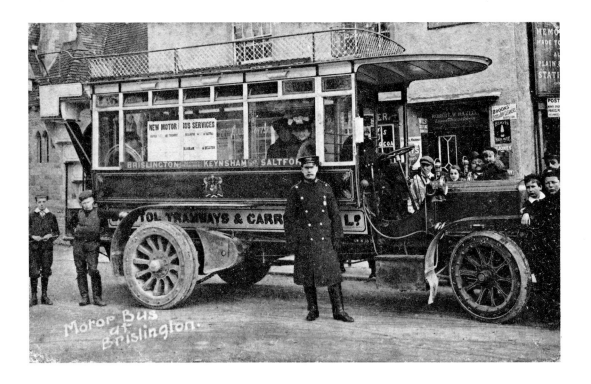

110. About 1906. Outside the post office in The Square at Brislington. An Act of Parliament of 1904 authorised an extension of the electric tramways from Brislington to Keynsham which if implemented could have led to a connection with the Bath tramways at Newton St. Loe via Saltford. These powers were never used and instead a motor-bus service from Brislington to Saltford commenced on 5th February 1906. The service was extended to Newton St. Loe on 20th August 1906 thus completing a road passenger service by bus and tram between Bristol and Bath. The motor-bus illustrated is a Thorneycroft chain driven single decker with staircase. Overhanging branches on the roads, steep hills and anxiety concerning the top-heavy appearance of the buses subsequently put a temporary stop to the use of seats, which were placed on top decks in 1909. All buildings behind the bus have since been demolished.

Stapleton Road Station, Bristol. 40.

111. Stapleton Road Station was opened on 8th September 1863; it was closed to goods services on 29th November 1965 and partially unstaffed on 16th June 1969. Work on the line from Temple Meads via Stapleton Road to New Passage Pier had started in October 1858, the purpose being to provide a link to South Wales via a passenger ferry to Portskewett Pier where there was a further rail connection to the South Wales lines. Prior to this it was necessary to travel via Gloucester. The opening of the Severn Tunnel on 1st December 1886 completed the rail link. In July 1887 all main passenger services from London to South Wales began using the route via a spur constructed to the east of Temple Meads station. The Clifton Extension Railway, which was opened to passengers on 1st October 1885, linked the Bristol Port Railway in the Avon Gorge to the Ashley Hill area, via a tunnel under Clifton Down. There was a link to Stapleton Road station at Narroways Hill.

Eastville, Bristol. 5.

112. About 1915. Stapleton Road, Eastville, looking from Robertson Road with Fishponds Road off to the right. On the extreme right can be seen the entrance to the Methodist Church built in 1877 at a cost of nearly £4,000. It could seat 500 persons, this figure being increased to 750 in 1901 as the result of internal alterations. The church was closed in 1971 and the site has been redeveloped with a modern office block. The houses in Stapleton Road beyond the lamp post were demolished for the M32 motorway flyover. From June 1876 a horse tram service ran from Old Market to Eastville. The route was electrified on 1st February 1897 and extended to the Full Moon Hotel, Fishponds, on 28th September 1897. Trams were abandoned on this line on 3rd September 1938.

The Union, Eastville, Bristol.
1456.

113. Unions of Parishes were formed in England and Wales for providing for the maintenance of the poor, on the passing of the Poor Law Amendment Act of 1834. However, Bristol had already obtained authority for the election of a Board of Guardians and the raising of a rate from a group of parishes in order to fund the maintenance of the destitute by a local Act of 1696. The Clifton Union (afterwards Barton Regis) was constituted under the 1834 Act and the parishes it covered were included in the City boundary by the extension of 1837. The Workhouse and administrative offices of the Barton Regis Union, built in 1860, were at 100, Fishponds Road, Eastville, shown here about 1917. After 1897 a new Union was formed for the whole of this area of the city. The workhouse at Eastville became an old persons home after the Second World War and was demolished in 1972. A development of council houses known as East Park has been built on the site and the surrounding grounds.

York Series. Fishponds Road. Eastville. 360.

114. Much of Eastville consists of solid working class housing of the Victorian and Edwardian era. The main road shown traversing the area leads to Fishponds; to the left is Freemantle Road, to the right is Berkeley Street. The shops on the left, nearest the bridge, were purpose built as such; with their steep gables and fancy barge boards they almost seem to be stone imitations of Tudor timber framed houses. The properties on the Fishponds Road frontage are grander and in places more rural in appearance than those built in the numerous side roads which lead off it. In order to pass under the railway bridge, special low height trams were purchased. The bridge has been removed following the closure of this section of railway line, and the road was widened after the cutting back of the embankment on either side. In the background rise the trees of Eastville Park with its main entrance at the junction with Muller Road.

STAPLETON RD & EASTVILLE PARK

115. At the junction of Stapleton Road and Glenfrome Road (off to the right) stood the old Mill House which was constructed in 1650. Between 1774 and 1867 the building was used as a Turnpike house; finally it became a shop selling refreshments and was demolished in 1929. Behind the oncoming horse and cart was a two arched bridge over the river Froom. The bridge was rebuilt also in 1929. In the distance can be seen the railway arches which used to span Stapleton Road. The land on the right behind the Mill House was residentially developed at the turn of the last century; the lower entrance of Eastville Park emerged onto Stapleton Road on the far side of the bridge. The M32 motorway now runs down from Purdown and an elevated section continues into the distance towards the junction with Muller Road.

EASTVILLE PARK BRISTOL. 573.

116. Bristol lagged behind many cities in accepting responsibility for the provision of open spaces. However, the Royal Family were actively involved in encouraging the public park movement and the City Council agreed to purchase seventy acres of land at Eastville for £30,000 from Sir J. Greville Symthe, the purchase being completed on 24th April 1888. The boating lake was constructed under the provisions of the Unemployed Workman's Act 1905 which authorised local authorities to create employment opportunities by means of schemes that would benefit the community. The boathouse on the edge of the lake replaced an earlier building which was burnt down by suffragettes. During the First World War the boating lake was extensively used for recreational purposes by the soldiers on leave or recuperating in one of the many war hospitals.

117. About 1926. The junction of Muller Road and Stapleton Road Eastville. In the distance is Ingmire Road branching off to the left. Houses were built in the 1930's in the gap site; some have since been demolished. There is now an entrance into the Eastville Stadium behind the bridge parapet beyond the policeman standing on the left-hand pavement. The bus waiting to cross the junction is an 'A' type, introduced in 1925, fitted with a 32 seat full fronted bus body. Its appearance led to its nickname the 'crab'. Only 23 'A' type chassis were built, four of them being fitted with single deck bodies. The shop premises, the houses behind them, and the houses on the front right have been demolished for the M32 fly-over, a roundabout, and a pedestrian underpass.

118. About 1904. Lodge Causeway, Fishponds; Russell Road off to the right which led to the edge of a large clay pit serving the Hollybrook Brick Works. The pit has now been grassed over and the brick works removed. In the distance the junction with Charlton Road, and Lodge Hill leading on from the Causeway. To the left is open ground subsequently laid out with roads and red brick semi-detached council houses in the early 1920's. The large houses on the right have been demolished and replaced with modern properties. This whole area was part of Kingswood Forest and the Causeway was a track which cut through the forest in a straight line. 'Lodge' is a reference to a hunting lodge traditionally associated with King John.

FISHPONDS RD. BRISTOL

119. Fishponds Road looking towards the 'Full Moon' Hotel about 1907. To the right is Station Road and to the left Hinton Road. Fishponds was once known as 'New Pools', the pools being situated in the vicinity of the 'Full Moon'. The trees mark the site of Beechwood, a large house owned by the Robinson family and demolished in 1934. The post office and a petrol filling station now occupy this area. The shelter in the road, built for the use of the tramways staff, has been removed. The electric trams reached this area in 1897 extending as far out as Staple Hill in September of the same year. To the right the low level buildings were demolished and the Vandyck Cinema, now a Social Club and Bingo Hall, built about 1927.

The Straits Fishpond's

120. Fishponds Road looking towards Downend Road and Staplehill Road along the section known as 'The Straits'. In the distance can be seen the Cross Hands Hotel which still stands at the fork in the road. The trees on the right have been removed, the avenue behind them forming the new pavement onto which front the gardens of the previously concealed stone built houses. The wall and trees on the left hand side formed the boundary of land which lay around Oldbury Court, a mansion owned by the Vassall family from 1833 onwards. The grounds were used for fairs and other events; in the 1930's the trees and wall were removed and the land was developed with houses and shops. The latter do not front Fishponds Road itself but were set back on Straits Parade.

Salutation Inn, Henbury.

Snitch, The Library, Westbury-on-Trym.

121. The Salutation Inn, Henbury, looking up Henbury Hill to the left. In front is the ford across the Hen, and to the left of the telegraph pole is Crow Lane. The inn, looking very much as it did in Victorian times, altered very little by the 1930's. A petrol pump was installed in the forecourt to cater for the advent of the motor car, the nearer of the two large trees was cut down and the post and rail fence and the adjacent footpath disappeared. The post war development of Henbury brought blocks of flats, swimming baths, shopping centre and schools to this rural area and Crow Lane has since been widened. The Salutation Inn has now been demolished and set back from the position shown, behind a large forecourt.

BAPTIST CHAPEL & GLOUCESTER RD. HORFIELD.

122. Gloucester Road, Horfield, looking towards the City about 1905. On the left the twin towers of the Gothic style Baptist Chapel built in 1900 at a cost of some £8,500. Seating accommodation was available for 1,100 people. The structures in the centre on top of each tower have been removed and the building has been extended by further construction on the sites of the first three houses to the right of the frontage of the chapel. Several of the houses further down the road have been converted to shopping/commercial use, resulting in alterations to the facade and the loss of the front garden and boundary walls. The Wesleyan Methodist Church can be seen in the distance on the corner of Wesley Road. It was opened in January 1894. The spire on the horizon is on the David Thomas Memorial Church, named after the first minister of Highbury Chapel.

KELLAWAY AVENUE
HORFIELD · BRISTOL · 244 ·

123. Horfield Common has been in use as common land for several hundred years. There were once two ponds in existence which may have provided fish for the monastery of St. Augustine (now the Cathedral) which owned the Manor of Horfield. In the background can be seen part of the Edwardian ribbon development along the main Gloucester Road, which borders the common. Horfield became densely populated with the building of large public and private housing estates in the 1920's and 1930's. Kellaway Avenue was opened on 23rd November 1920 by the Postmaster-General, Mr. F.G. Kellaway MP, who was born in the district. The trees have since grown considerably and the workman's hut has been removed. When the military barracks were built on the edge of the common, the officers were specifically warned not to ride their horses over the land.

124. About 1916. A view on part of the common opposite Horfield Barracks, used as a drill and sports ground. Horfield is spelt as Horefelle in the Domesday Book, and the area was once heavily forested. The men are recruits for the Gloucester Regiment, still in their civilian clothes. Until January 1916 enrolment into the armed forces was voluntary. Then single men from the age of 18 to 41 were required to enlist. By June 1916 enlistment was extended to married men aged 18 to 41, followed by June 1918 to all men aged 18 to 48 who were not otherwise engaged in war work. The wall of the barracks can be seen behind the two men on the extreme left of the picture. The foundation stone was laid on 3rd June 1845 and the building cost £57,000. It was occupied as the Depot of the Gloucester Regiment and headquarters of the 28th Regimental District. The buildings were demolished in 1966.

125. Bristol Tramways and Carriage Company's electric tram
No. 40 outside Horfield Barracks about 1917. The Horfield
tramway opened on 18th November 1880 using steam
traction built by the Hughes Locomotive and Tramway
Company Ltd. Although a success from the practical point of
view the noisy engines frightened horses and other domestic
animals, and both passengers on the trailer and the owners of
property along the route complained of noise, dirt and
fumes. After a year, horses took over the route which initially terminated at Egerton Road and was then extended to
Horfield in 1892. The line was electrified in 1900 and
extended to Filton Church on 21st March 1907. Tram No. 40
came into service in 1900. It was the standard type used in
Bristol seating 24 passengers inside on two longitudinal
benches and 29 passengers on top, on seats with hinged
covers which could be tipped in wet weather to reveal a dry
side.

NEW ESTATE, FILTON ROAD, HORFIELD.

COPYRIGHT
HRFD. 9.

LILYWHITE LTD.,
TRIANGLE. HALIFAX.

126. About 1927. Filton Road Horfield, looking away from the City with St. Gregory's Road off to the right where the children are standing. The tram is heading for Filton village on a line extended there from Horfield Barracks in 1907. This tram route was abandoned on 15th July 1939. Initially 74½ acres of land on which the Horfield Estate is built was acquired by the City Council in 1919 at a cost of £15,540. By 1930 the total area acquired had increased to 149 acres at a cost of £33,960 and 1,520 houses had been built or were in the course of construction. Weekly rent and rates were 11/6 for a non-parlour type three bedroom house and 13/- for a parlour type. The density of the houses on the Council Estates was limited to twelve to the acre at this time in order to provide well planned houses with ample gardens. A distance of 75 feet was maintained between houses on opposite sides of a road to ensure the maximum amount of sunlight.

Tram Terminus, Knowle Bristol

A.G.S. & Cº. 311.

127. The tram terminus on the Wells Road Knowle, outside the 'Red Lion' public house about 1915. Tram No. 208 on route No. 10 from Bristol Bridge via Temple Meads Station, has arrived from the direction of the City, nearest the camera. The other route on the line was No. 15 which ran from Knowle to Hanham via Old Market. Knowle was once spelt without the 'e'. It was part of the parish of Bedminster and in a short space of time at the turn of the century it grew from a rural to a suburban area. Even so, in 1915 the houses on the right marked the end of the ribbon development on that side of Wells Road; beyond the public house there were only some ten houses and then open country as far as the village of Whitchurch. This open area has since been filled with urban development.

(2) LAWRENCE HILL, BRISTOL.

128. Lawrence Hill, viewed from the brige over the now disused Midland Railway line between Bristol and Birmingham. On the right between the advertising hoardings was Berkeley Street leading to the Bristol Wagon and Carriage Works Co., Ltd., 'makers of landaulette and motor car bodies of all kinds to suit customers own chassis'. To the left of the building advertising Diadem flour, the end of Leadhouse Road and Croydon Street. The rank of shops on the right was once the headquarters of the Bristol and District Co-operative Society Ltd. which in 1905 had fourteen branches on the north side of the River Avon, and a membership of 8,000. The tower and spire are of the church of St. Lawrence which was consecrated on 17th September 1885. It stood near the spot where there was once the chapel of a leper hospital dedicated to St. Lawrence. Everything illustrated except the bridge has been demolished and the site is occupied by road improvements and council housing.

The Bishop's Palace, Bristol.

129. The Bishops Palace at the rear of the Cathedral was looted and destroyed by fire in the Bristol Riots of 1831. The Bishopric of Bristol was amalgamated with Gloucester in 1836, but in 1877 moves were made to separate it again; the raising of the necessary endowment took twenty years and the revival of the See of Bristol necessitated the provision of an Episcopal Palace. Such a building had been built at Stapleton in the 1850's but not being used it was sold and became Colston's School. A new Palace was therefore built at a cost of about £14,000 on the edge of Redland Green, close to what in now Redland Court Road. The Palace was gutted in an air-raid on 2nd December 1940; the ruins were used during the making of a film illustrating the rescue services in 1942 and have since been grassed over.

Orthopaedic Hospital
Redland, Bristol

130. The Orthopaedic Hospital and Home for crippled children was established in Grove Road, Redland in 1876. It provided an education for those children who because of disability would not otherwise have attended school. The house could accommodate thirty-five children who were given a diet of good food and fresh air plus medical attention. Boys were transferred to the Kensington home when they reached the age of ten; the girls could stay until they reached the age of fourteen after which they would go straight into suitable employment. Relief of the sick and suffering was heavily dependent on charity and voluntary assistance. Relatively wealthy 'patrons' took an interest in institutions such as the Home and children were assisted during their stay and subsequent period of training for a trade by individuals who 'adopted' them. The building is now used as a day hospital and clinic.

Bowling Green.
St. Andrews Park. Bristol.

131. Before the advent of purpose built parks, the public, or rather those of the public who had the leisure time and the means of getting there, relied on parades, churchyards, squares and common land for their open-air recreation. Apart from the acquisition of the Downs in 1861 little was done to provide open space for public use until the late 1880's. As the urban areas developed it was necessary to ensure that some provision was made for recreation. The City Council acquired eleven acres of land in 1890 which was laid out as St. Andrews Park and opened on 1st May 1895 for the benefit of the expanding suburbs of Horfield and Montpelier. Bowling enjoyed a revival of popularity in the 1900's. The houses are in Melita and Sommerville Roads.

Higher Grade School, St George.

132. St. George Higher Grade School, Church Road, was one of three schools (including Fairfield and Merrywood) built to provide education of wider scope and of higher standard than that given in the elementary schools. The higher grade schools set a new standard not only in education, but in building, equipment and staffing. They were declared illegal because they provided secondary education supported by the rates, but subsequently became reputable local authority grammar schools. The Education Act 1902 abolished the old School Boards and provided for primary and secondary education to be administered by Town and County Councils. St. George first opened in November 1894; in 1906 the fees were £1 per annum, with a number of free places filled each year by competition. Secondary education for all did not come until 1944. The old smithy and the houses on the left have been demolished.

St. George Church & Fountain

Sutherland, Redfield

133. The fountain, St. George. Clouds Hill Road to the left and Summerhill Road to the right. In 1728 a shoemaker who had committed suicide was reputedly buried here at dead of night with a stake through his heart. However, the body was apparently dug up and sold to surgeons for dissection. The original St. George's Church was consecrated in 1756 by Bishop Hume. At the time a large part of Kingswood lay in the parish of St. Philip and St. Jacob, but the existing parish church was remote from the large number of colliers working in the area. Accordingly St. George's Church was built to meet their needs, being the first local church built for 300 years. It was rebuilt in 1846 and destroyed by fire in 1878. The church illustrated was opened in 1880 and demolished 15th July 1976. Horse trams ran from Old Market to St. George from October 1876. The line was extended to Kingswood in 1892 and electrified in 1895. The St. George-Hanham line went electric in 1900.

Sea Mills Station

134. Sea Mills Station was opened on 6th March 1865, as part of the Bristol Port Railway and Pier Company line built in anticipation of the development of shipping business at Avonmouth. The Clifton Extension Railway which opened in 1874, linked the system into the general rail network but the disputed cost of a signalling station at Sneyd Park junction delayed the use of the new line for passenger traffic beyond Clifton Down Station until September 1885. At first there was only a single track through to Avonmouth Station; with the increase in dock traffic this was doubled in 1906. It was necessary to construct a new steel bridge over the stream at Sea Mills and improvements were carried out to the station itself. Hadrian Close temporary bungalows were built near to the station in the late 1940's and the construction of the Portway and surrounding roads has taken away much of the rural atmosphere.

Coombe Dale, Sea Mills Park

PHOTO
HEPWORTH.

135. Coombe Dale looking towards Dingle View about 1928. Bounded on the northern side by the wooded slopes of Kingsweston Down and on the south-west by the river Avon, Sea Mills Park is the most picturesquely situated of all the City Council housing estates. The houses shown were erected in 1926-1927. In order to overcome difficulties regarding shortage of materials and labour a number of forms of construction other than brick were used, these particular houses being of the 'Dorman Long' system (steel frame and concrete). By 31st March 1930, 1,252 houses had been erected or were in the course of construction on the estate and the cost of construction per unit had fallen from £1,052 in 1920 to £390 in 1930.

136. About 1920. The Three Lamps Junction, Totterdown, coming out of Bristol with Bath Road off to the left and Wells Road off to the right. With the exception of the wall covered with advertisements, everything which can be seen has been demolished. The road junction has since been widened and the finger post situated at the apex of the junction has been replaced having been removed to the City Council's yard in Dovercourt Road pending the completion of the road works. Everyone, male and female, can be seen wearing a hat; to judge by the general movement of the pedestrians and the number of passengers on the tram leaving the city, it is early evening, and the public are returning home from work or the shops. Hayman's furniture stores which are advertised above the building in the centre of the picture were at No. 66, Castle Street, near the junction with Queen Street.

Totterdown.   Bristol.

137. Wells Road, Totterdown, looking towards the City about 1906. On the right-hand side No. 96 W. Goodall and Sons, bootmakers, next door are Hodders the chemist; the horse and open cart are stood outside of the Totterdown sub-post office. Behind the cart is Sims the grocers. On the left-hand side is the Phoenix Hotel on the corner of Bush Street with a Pickfords disinfecting lorry (horse-drawn) waiting to enter the main road. Tram No. 87 has come from the 'Red Lion' at Knowle and its journey will terminate at Bristol Bridge via Temple Meads, referred to at that time as the Joint Station as it was used by more than one of the railway companies which existed prior to British Railways. Totterdown was one of the large residential suburban areas which was built to deal with the increase in Bristol's population. Everything in the picture was demolished in the early 1970's for road improvements most of which were later abandoned; the modified scheme is only now nearing completion.

138. Victoria or Windmill Hill Park was formally opened in 1891, the land having been bought by the Council in 1888. The brick walls on the left surround the open-air baths which existed at the Hill Avenue/St. Lukes Road junction of the park. Below the horizon stand the houses in the Bushey Park area which were demolished in the 1970's. Ravenhill Road has been built through the open country to the right. Totterdown was urbanised in the latter part of the nineteenth century with the building of working class houses. These climbed over the brow of the hill instead of along its contours. The streets dropped down a sharply inclined slope and were some of the steepest in the south of England. Totterdown was therefore an apt description as well as a name.

WESTBURY HILL.

139. Westbury Hill, Westbury-on-Trym about 1910. At the bottom of the hill can be seen the still undeveloped area opposite Mogfords shop. Coming back up the hill the turning to the right is Waters Lane leading to Eastfield Road. Nearest the camera and to the left is Cambridge Crescent with Stuckeys Bank (later Parrs) on the corner. Tram No's. 1 and 4 entered service in 1900, although the route to Westbury was not opened until 1908. No. 4 is heading for the Tramways Centre via Redland Green. The Westbury trams were the first to go in the changeover to buses, and the last tram on this route ran on 7th May 1938. The next day the overhead wire had been removed as far as Whiteladies Road.

TRAMWAY TERMINUS. WESTBURY.

140. The tramway terminus at Westbury-on-Trym about 1910. The extension of the tram service from Durdham Down to Westbury was the final stage of the tramways expansion, the section from White Tree to the Jubilee fountain coming into use on 28th October 1908. An Act of Parliament of 1904 had given the Tramways Company the authority to extend the track further from the village to Henbury (the Salutation Inn) but these proposals were never implemented. The fountain in the centre of the picture was erected in June 1897 by the parishioners of Westbury to commemorate Queen Victoria's Diamond Jubilee. It was removed to Canford Park in 1920 and the present War Memorial was built in its place. The trees have been removed and the land developed with shops and a post office.